# Empire Bank

*Come bank with a friend.*

# Crossroads at the Spring

A Pictorial History of Springfield, Missouri
by The History Museum
for Springfield-Greene County

edited by
Shanna Boyle and Julie March

A rainy day in the 1920s at the corner of St. Louis Street and Jefferson Avenue shows the corner of the Woodruff Building at the far right.

THE
DONNING COMPANY
PUBLISHERS

# DEDICATION

*This book is dedicated to the collection, preservation, and exhibition of our community's rich and unique heritage which has made this book possible.*

*All proceeds from the sale of this book will go to benefit the History Museum for Springfield-Greene County.*

The Donning Company/Publishers
184 Business Park Drive, Suite 106
Virginia Beach, VA 23462

Steve Mull, General Manager
Nancy Schneiderheinze, Project Director
Paula A. Ridge, Project Research Coordinator
Sally C. Davis, Associate Editor
Percival J. Tesoro, Graphic Designer
Dawn V. Kofroth, Assistant General Manager
Tony Lillis, Director of Marketing
Teri S. Arnold, Marketing Coordinator

Library of Congress Cataloging-in-Publication Data

Crossroads at the spring: a pictorial history of Springfield,
Missouri/by the History Museum for Springfield-Greene
County; edited by Shanna Boyle and Julie March.
p.    cm.
Includes bibliographical references and index.
ISBN 1-57864-015-6 (alk. paper)
1. Springfield (Mo.)—History—Pictorial works.  I. Boyle, Shanna, 1966–, II. March, Julie, 1944–    .
III. History Museum for Springfield-Greene County (Springfield, Mo.)
F474.S7C76   1997
977.8'78—dc21
97-28910
CIP

Printed in the United States of America

**End sheet:**
Springfield's downtown bustled in 1925 as automobiles and electric streetcars transported citizens over brick streets. John T. Woodruff's Colonial Hotel is pictured on the right at the southwest corner of Jefferson Avenue and St. Louis Street on Route 66. Built in 1907, the Colonial Hotel was the first fireproof building in the Ozarks and also offered a number of specialty shops, a barber shop, a telegraph office, and a coffee shop cooled by refrigerated air.

# TABLE OF CONTENTS

SUITS MADE TO ORDER $15.-35.
'MET' TAILOR SHOP
JOHN SCHIBLER. TAILOR
PHONE 982
CLEANING-PRESSING-REPAIRING.

AGENCY
LEWIS LAUNDRY

316
TAILOR
SHOP

CLEANING
PRESSING
REPAIRING

SUITS PRESSED
While U Wait.
SHOE SHINE

SUITS made to ORDER
$15.00 to $35.00

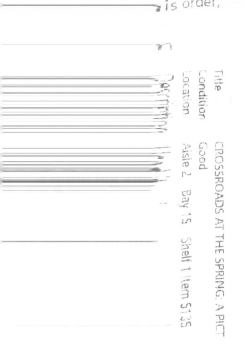

# and Acknowledgments

his book was an opportunity we have looked forward to for
cellent way of sharing some of the wonderful photographs
's Archives and to celebrate our community's heritage. As
ed the difficulty of choosing only 220 photographs from
hives. The photographs in this book identify many of the
people that have been a part of Springfield's history. Our
presentation of the community. It was with great difficul-
hs were eliminated from this book. We sincerely tried to
ble and give a fair representation of our community.

members of the Book Committee who spent endless hours
d performing the many other tasks needed to produce a
pictorial history book. These dedicated individuals are: Hayward Barnett, Patsy Corbett,
Rex Edmonson, Ken Elkins, Jean Fulbright, Richard Grosenbaugh, Beth Snow and Holly
Bowdidge Stone.

We also wish to thank Empire Bank and Mike Williamson for sponsoring the book
and making this project possible.

Finally, a special thanks to Wayne Bartee for reading and offering suggestions on the
book manuscript, to Picture This for excellent photograph reproductions and Springfield
Blueprint for quality copies. There are many other people we would like to thank who
aided with research, locating information or other guidance. These are: The Shepard
Room (Michael Glenn, Sharol Neely, Bettie Hickman, John Rutherford and Lisa
Cameron), Bob Chancellor, Lisa Arnall-Young, Charles Sheppard, and Robert Neumann.

Some of the photographs in this book include unidentified people or places. If any-
one should recognize an unidentified person or place, please contact the History
Museum. When writing this book we included only the information deemed accurate at
the time.

We would like to thank the many people who have supported the History Museum
and donated photographs to the Archives. Your contributions have made this book possible.

*Shanna Boyle and Julie March*

**Left:**
**The Met Tailor Shop was located
at 316 College Street circa 1915.
Pictured are (right) tailor John
Schibler with Shorty Gregory.**

Farming in the Ozarks could be hard work as shown by the rocky soil in this photograph.

# Ga

### ᴖᏩ᠇ᏦᏬ

Much of southwest Missouri is part of the Ozark Highlands, a region of more than ten thousand sparkling springs. This abundant water supply, along with good soil on the Springfield plateau, led to human settlements as early as 10,000 B.C. These prehistoric peoples were hunters and gatherers whom we know through their distinctive stone tools and weapons.

Through the centuries these groups evolved into Native American tribes, and what was to become Springfield began as a crossroads of trails.

The Osage tribe dominated southwest Missouri by the period of European exploration in the early 1700s. The Osage were described by John James Audubon as "well formed, athletic and robust men of noble aspect." Osage domination ended in the early 1800s when southwest Missouri became a dumping ground for displaced tribes from east of the Mississippi River. White settlers were demanding land on the frontier, and the Delaware, Kickapoo and Shawnee were crowded into what would become Taney, Christian and Greene counties. By 1832 all the tribes had signed treaties that led to their removal to reservations in Kansas Territory.

A circa 1890 map of Greene County shows early roads and Indian trails, villages and mounds. This illustration was drawn by A. M. Haswell for Fairbanks and Tuck, *Past and Present of Greene County, Missouri.*

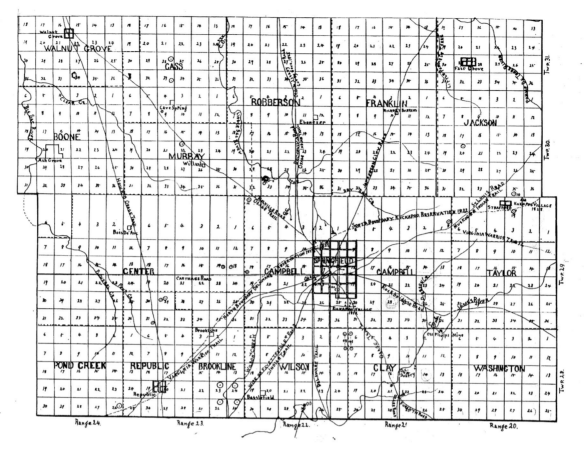

Left:
Tisnytianka, a Little Osage Indian chief, was photographed on a Kansas reservation in 1877. Photograph courtesy of the Kansas State Historical Society, Topeka, Kansas.

Left:
Two unidentified young Osage women, one holding a small child on her lap, are representative of the first Native Americans in this area. Photograph courtesy of the Kansas State Historical Society, Topeka, Kansas.

Right:
This 1830 watercolor by George Catlin depicts a Delaware Indian named Nicoman (meaning "the answer"). Reproduced with permission of the Gilcrease Museum, Tulsa, Oklahoma.

White settlement began in 1818 when John Pettijohn made a claim and built a cabin on the James River in what is now Greene County. When Missouri became a state in 1821, it was on the edge of the frontier, bordered on the west by the vast lands known as Indian Territory. Aggressive young pioneers from Tennessee, Kentucky and North Carolina were looking for new, productive land following leads from Henry Rowe Schoolcraft and other explorers. Schoolcraft wrote of the Springfield plain, "The lands consist of rich black alluvial soil, apparently deep and calculated for corn, flax and hemp."

One of these aggressive young pioneers was John Polk Campbell from Maury County, Tennessee who came through southwest Missouri in the mid–1820s seeking new and fertile land. According to family legend, Campbell cured a Kickapoo Indian boy while staying on the James River. This earned him a tract of land to the north, near what was later called the Natural Well.

Campbell, his family, and slaves returned in March of 1830 to establish their home on this land and found the William Fulbright and A. J. Burnett families living here also. Joseph Rountree and his family, also from Maury County, Tennessee, arrived shortly thereafter and settled near the already established families. These families were community builders who aspired to create a town where they and their descendants could make their homes.

As in other pioneer communities, the first homes of these settlers were log cabins with dirt floors; their slaves lived in cloth tents. Land was cleared around the area which is now the public square, and crops were planted in fields that had been cultivated by the Kickapoo Indians. The town was probably first called Campbell and Fulbright Springs. It was said that John Polk Campbell and his wife, Louisa, built and vacated thirteen cabins in the first year in order to make room for newcomers.

The first store was opened in 1831 by Junius Campbell, and other necessary businesses were established: dry goods, blacksmiths, millers, and cabinet makers. In 1831 the first log schoolhouse opened with Joseph Rountree as teacher. Itinerant preachers had been visiting the area, and in 1833 a church was built. By this time, at least one hundred families had settled in the crossroads at the spring which was still quite isolated with the nearest post office one hundred miles away.

On January 2, 1833, Greene County was created and named after Revolutionary War hero Nathanael Greene. John Polk Campbell was appointed county clerk, and his brother, Junius, was appointed county treasurer. The following year Junius was appointed the first postmaster.

**Right:**
The majority of African Americans came to Missouri as slaves, brought by their white owners as they moved west. This former slave, whose name has been lost, belonged to the John G. Perryman family. She stayed with the family after emancipation and lived out her life with them.

Louisa Terrill Cheairs came to the new frontier settlement with her husband John Polk Campbell as a bride of seventeen. She bore ten children, nine of them in Springfield, and at her husband's death in 1853, became the sole owner of their extensive property.

Mary Frances Campbell Sproul, born in 1831, was the second child of Louisa and John Polk Campbell and the first white girl born in Springfield.

By 1835 the name Campbell and Fulbright Springs had been changed to Springfield. Campbell succeeded in having Springfield named the county seat of Greene County by deeding to the town fifty acres of land centered around the public square. In 1838 Springfield was incorporated and had a population of about three hundred.

In the next two decades, citizens concentrated their energies on business and education. May of 1845 saw the opening of the first bank, a branch of the Missouri State Bank. Johnson and Wilson Company carried a full line of fall and winter dry goods, groceries, hardware, boots, shoes, books and stationery. They would sell these for cash or produce such as beeswax, tallow, hemp, furs and pelts. J. D. Haden built a mill and distillery and sold whiskey by the barrel. Described by one local as "that curse of America," whiskey provoked a strong temperance backlash in the 1840s.

**The marriage of John Nathaniel Campbell and Mary Danforth in 1854 brought together two wealthy and influential Springfield families.**

**Left:**
**Celia Sheppard, formerly a slave of the Henry Sheppard family, posed for this picture at the southwest corner of Hampton Avenue and St. Louis Street in 1902.**

**Below Right:**
**The second plat of Springfield shows the fifty acre tract deeded by John Polk and Louisa Campbell to Greene County. The map is dated 1867 because the original plat burned in an 1861 courthouse fire.**

**Above:**
**Samuel Fulbright, the seventh of nine sons of William and Ruth Fulbright, settled with his family at a spring on Jordan Creek in 1829. As Greene County sheriff, he was executioner at the county's first legal hanging in 1854, the first of only two in Greene County.**

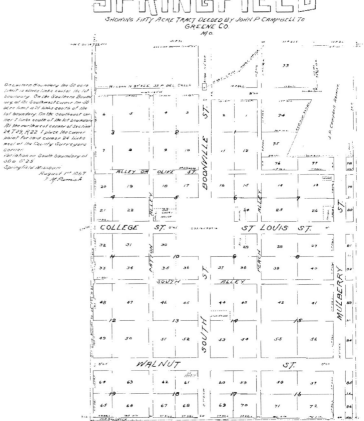

Several small, private schools were opened and solicited for pupils in the *Springfield Advertiser*, one of several short-lived newspapers. The Springfield Academy (also known as Stephens Academy), started in 1845 by J. A. Stephens, offered male students five months of school for $7.50 in tuition. Carlton College opened in 1848 as the first all-female academy but soon became co-educational.

Law and order was also a concern. The town's first constable was appointed in 1849, and by 1858 Springfield had its first police department with a marshall and two officers.

By 1850 settlers had carved out many farms and produced wheat, pork, and potatoes, bred and sold horses and mules; they also had opened a wide variety of shops. Springfield provided drug stores, cabinet and furniture shops, blacksmithing and tin shops, saddle, harness and wagon shops for its population of twelve hundred. There were two newspapers, tailors, milliners, shoe shops, a gunsmith and livery stable, a land office and a bank. The town was served by ten lawyers, five doctors, one dentist and four clergymen. All this developed without access to railroad or steamboat transportation.

**Left:**
**Physician, surveyor, and landowner Horatio Monroe Parrish came to Greene County from Kentucky in the late 1830s. He drew the 1867 Springfield plat showing the Campbells' land grant.**

**William Marion Weaver, a descendant of the pioneering Fulbright family, became a seventeen-year-old bugler in Company G, Third Missouri Volunteers during the 1846 war with Mexico.**

**The forced march of Cherokees from Tennessee and Georgia to Oklahoma included one route which passed through Springfield in 1838. The Cherokees called it *Nuna-da-el-tsun-yi* or "the trail on which they cried." This painting by Robert Lidneux is reproduced with permission of the Wooloroc Museum in Bartlesville, Oklahoma.**

This view of the public square, looking northwest toward Boonville Avenue, shows Springfield's first bank, a branch of the Missouri State Bank.

The Bell Tower was in the center of the public square as seen looking down South Avenue in 1876.

The southeast corner of Springfield's public square, circa 1859, supported a variety of businesses. This is the earliest known photograph of the town.

Carriages and streetcars gathered for an unidentified turn-of-the-century event at the northeast corner of the public square, which was destroyed by fire in 1913.

The concrete "pie," first installed in 1913, was removed in 1947 to provide more parking on the public square.

Above:
The second Greene County Courthouse is featured in the center of this view of the public square and College Street, circa 1895. The tallest building to the right, Baker Block, held Springfield's first elevator.

The Springfield Chamber of Commerce was located at Walnut Street and Jefferson Avenue in 1921. Guaranty Federal Savings Bank at 330 East Walnut Street now stands on this site. The Chamber of Commerce is now located at the southeast corner of John Q. Hammons Parkway and St. Louis Street.

# 2

## Taming the Frontier

Springfield and Greene County have often enjoyed growth and prosperity since the 1830s. City and county political leaders have contributed to this progress in generally constructive ways and have led local government through several periods of crisis.

Before the Civil War, Greene County government overshadowed Springfield economically and politically. The Greene County Court first met in the John Polk Campbell home in 1833, two years before the state officially recognized Springfield as a community. The County's first official building, the courthouse, opened in 1837 while Springfield's government did not find a permanent home until 1938.

Granting relief to the county's first pauper in 1833 as well as the first homicide in 1836, were signs of a growing community. There were many marriages, some fifty divorces, and numerous civil cases in the two decades before the Civil War. These events kept county officials busy and suggest that early Greene County citizens were sometimes contentious.

Springfield incorporated in 1838 and was governed by a loosely organized board of trustees that sometimes failed to meet. Nicholas Smith chaired this board in 1847, and the town elected other city officials and a city council. By 1860 the county's population had grown to approximately thirty-five hundred of which nearly two thousand lived in Springfield.

During the Civil War conventional warfare in southwest Missouri was overshadowed by the brutal guerilla war that dominated the region and left a bitter legacy. County and city government were suspended during the war, leaving the area under military control.

The years following the war were a time of change, uncertainty, and growth. In 1866 a vigilante group known as the Regulators took the law into their own hands and purged the county of wrongdoers. In 1867, Permilla Caroline Stephens became the first female postmaster. The Atlantic & Pacific railway construction was rapidly approaching, and city businessmen vied over the location of a depot. Substantial cash and donated land brought the railroad to newly created North Springfield in 1870. Further improvements included the first free mail delivery to the town in 1888.

The United States Customhouse and Post Office, a fine Richardsonian Romanesque limestone building, opened in 1894, largely a result of lobbying by Springfield's business and political leaders. A new nine miles-per-hour speed limit in 1903 indicated that automobiles were replacing horses and mules.

The current county courthouse, which opened in 1912, is located at Boonville Avenue and Central Street.

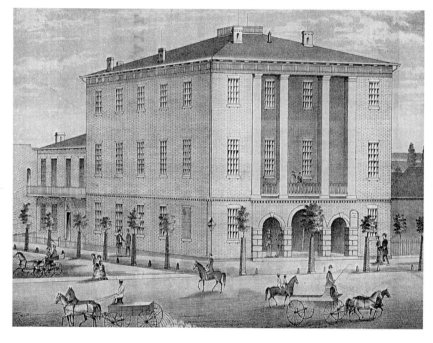

From its earliest meetings in the home of John Polk Campbell until 1838, the Greene County Court has moved to progressively larger facilities: the first, on the square, was destroyed by fire in 1861; the second, in this picture, stood on the northwest corner of the square until 1914.

Born and educated in Connecticut, John Smith Phelps came to Springfield in 1837 to practice law. A state legislator before the Civil War and Missouri governor during the 1870s, Phelps was one of the few area Democrats to hold office after the war. His wife, Mary Whitney Phelps, received $20,000 from the U.S. Congress after the war for meritorious service; she used the money to care for orphans of Union soldiers. This engraving is reprinted from Holcomb, *History of Greene County, Missouri*.

18

Not all changes were positive, however. The tragic lynchings of three black men on Easter weekend in 1906 led many blacks to flee the area in fear. The failure of local officials to control the mob or later convict those guilty of the crimes was sad proof that not all was well in the community as it moved into the new century.

Local concern about the effectiveness of city government combined with the national Progressive Movement led Springfield to adopt the mayor-commission form of government in 1915.

Prohibition in the 1920s proved to be nearly unenforceable. Racial prejudice continued as the local Ku Klux Klan rose to as many as three thousand active members. The effects of the Great Depression were countered by local government's implementation of several of Roosevelt's New Deal programs, primarily providing employment through construction of parks and public buildings.

The first jail used in Springfield was the Greene County Jail, donated to the county in 1834. Springfield's city council decided the city needed its own facility, and the calaboose (pictured here) was built in 1891 and used until 1957. It is currently being restored for use as a police sub-station and museum.

The colorful career of Sempronius Hamilton Boyd, nicknamed "Pony," included terms as Springfield's youngest mayor, Civil War service in the Union army, a stint in the U.S. House of Representatives and as Minister Resident and Consul-General to Siam. As Judge of the Missouri Fourteenth Judicial District, he presided at the 1865 Springfield manslaughter trial of James B. "Wild Bill" Hickock. Photograph courtesy of Jim Joplin.

The federal building was completed in 1894 and served as the United States Customhouse and Post Office until 1938, when it became the City Hall.

The mile between Springfield and North Springfield showed little commercial development in 1892. The photograph shows the future site of the U.S. Customhouse and Post Office, now historic City Hall.

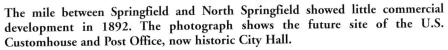

19

In 1938, however, a new federal building and post office, the H. S. Jewell Building, opened at Central Street and Boonville Avenue. City government offices then moved into the 1894 Customhouse and Post Office, and the building was renamed City Hall. In 1987 the main post office opened in the new Gene Taylor Building at Chestnut Expressway and Main Avenue. The city later purchased the Jewell Building, remodeled it for expanding city offices, and renamed it the Busch Municipal Building after Donald Busch, a former city manager.

By 1945 the City of Springfield controlled gas, electrical, and bus services and operated the Municipal Airport, now called the Downtown Airport, on East Division Street. The city opened the present-day airport, now called the Springfield-Branson Regional Airport, on July 2, 1945.

While World War II contracts fueled the local economy and set the stage for post-war prosperity, local government struggled to meet the needs of a swelling and increasingly diverse population.

The Springfield Library opened in 1903 and was funded by a $50,000 donation from the Carnegie Fund. In 1947 voters approved funding for a county library which merged with the city library in 1971. The Home Rule Charter Commission wrote a new city charter in 1952 creating a council-manager form of government. In 1953 nine city council members and a professional city manager were sworn in, and in 1979 the charter was amended to allow direct election of city mayors. Springfield's public facilities were gradually opened to all of its citizens following desegregation of the public schools in 1954.

**Left:**
Because of the common use of wood-framed structures, fire was a constant danger for the people of Springfield. The earliest voluntary fire fighters' organization was formed during the 1850s. After a disastrous fire in 1867, the Pride of the West Hook and Ladder Company was organized. Springfield's first paid fire department, however, was not established until 1896. These men were one of the earliest groups of professional fire fighters, circa 1897.

Springfield's first public library, constructed in 1903 near Springfield High School (now known as Central) was funded with $50,000 from the Carnegie Fund, part of a multi-million dollar philanthropic effort by the steel magnate Andrew Carnegie. The county library created in the late 1940s was later joined with the city library. This building now serves as the community's Main Library.

Postcards, such as this 1913 example, promoted Springfield as a desirable place to live.

During the Great Depression, President Roosevelt's New Deal programs and federal dollars put many Springfieldians to work building public works such as this swimming pool at Silver Springs Park. Others worked for the Historical Records Survey gathering information for church, city, and county histories.

Street lamps, first installed in 1867, gave way to Springfield Gas Works' fifty street lights in 1875. This was followed by conversion to electric lamps in 1886 by Springfield Gas and Electric Co. (shown in this 1920s photograph).

Originally created in 1928, the Springfield Art Museum received support from the city in 1946 through a levy by the city council and in 1958 moved to a new building in Phelps Grove Park where it is currently located. In 1957 the James River Power Station opened, and the city purchased the Springfield Water Company. In 1967 the Southwest Power Station was opened.

During our nation's bicentennial, citizens had a growing interest in preserving the heritage of the community. The Bicentennial Historical Museum of the Ozarks opened (now the History Museum for Springfield-Greene County), and historic sites boards registered historic properties.

Today, the struggle to preserve our community's heritage persists while political leaders continue working to meet the complex needs of the citizens.

City Utilities began construction of its new office building on Central Street in 1952. The Main Library is pictured behind the construction site.

Policeman Waidie Phillips served in the 1932 Springfield Police Department's Motorcycle Squad.

Regular mail delivery to Springfield began with the Butterfield Overland Mail coach in 1858. Service was interrupted by the Civil War but resumed on a greatly improved schedule when the railroad came in 1870. Mail was handled by the railroad post office until the late 1880s, and in 1888 the city received its first free mail delivery to the post office on the public square. Rural Free Delivery (R.F.D.) and parcel post came in 1913, and in 1929 the first air mail service was introduced. Mailman Fay Grier poses with a Christmas delivery in this photograph.

Billed as "the largest convention center in the Southwest," Springfield's Convention Hall opened in 1913. Located on the west side of South Campbell Avenue, between Walnut Street and College Street, the three-story hall hosted exhibitions, meetings, musical events, and the community Christmas tree. It was razed for a parking lot in 1958.

Other civic centers have been proposed for the city, such as this 1923 plan adjoining Old City Hall. All, however, have been turned down by voters.

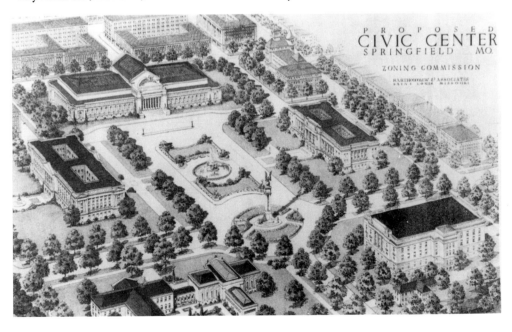

Queen City Stables stood at 307-311 West Walnut Street, circa 1885.

# 3

# Building a Community

From the beginning of white settlement, Springfield's economy was tied to agriculture, and the region's market center was on and around the public square. Dry goods stores, hardware stores, gunsmiths, blacksmiths, grocers and mills served the community's needs and used the crops produced on surrounding farms.

Farmers from miles around brought their produce to sell in Springfield. They sold wheat, corn, a variety of fruits and vegetables, beef cattle, hogs, poultry and dairy products. Business was good until the Civil War brought an end to nearly all commerce.

Within five years of the war's end, however, the southwest branch of the Atlantic & Pacific Railroad reached Springfield and brought an economic boom to the town. The 1880s marked the beginning of a growth period for Springfield, now nicknamed the Queen City of the Ozarks, as the population more than tripled in size by 1890. Prominent historians said, "During this decade, Springfield has at last thrown aside her swaddling clothes and started toward her destiny of becoming a metropolitan city."

The coming of the railroad also led to the creation of another community, North Springfield. The recommendations of a pre–Civil War survey and the wealth of several influential businessmen resulted in location of the railroad one mile north of the public square.

An eighty-foot-wide Commercial Street, the main street of North Springfield, was inviting to the many businesses that quickly grew in the area. Within a few years of the railroad's advent, there were four hundred homes, thirty businesses, and thirteen saloons in North Springfield. The division between the towns lasted seventeen years until, as described at the time, "some first class funerals lessened the ranks of the irreconcilables." In 1887 Springfield and North Springfield became one.

The Springfield Wagon Company opened for business in 1872, producing high quality farm-to-market wagons. After an 1883 fire, the factory relocated at the junction of the Frisco and Gulf railroads, tapping into a national market. By the 1890s the company led the Midwest market with its best-selling wagon dubbed, "The Old Reliable."

The Sunshine Mine, east of Springfield on Pearson Creek, produced lead and zinc in an area mined earlier by Native Americans.

In 1899 Boonville Avenue between the public square and Center Street (now Central) was lined with dozens of prosperous businesses.

The Springfield Brewing Company, also known as the Southwest Brewery, was owned and operated by German-born Sebastian Dingledein. At its peak in 1882 the brewery, at Fort Avenue and College Street, produced twenty-one hundred barrels of beer a day. Dingledein and his sons also owned and supplied a number of taverns in Springfield.

Dan King's Restaurant was on the southwest corner of Commercial Street and Benton Avenue along with Dan King's Saloon, Pool Hall, and a rooming house, called the Frisco House.

Popular photographer Harry Morgan captured hundreds of Springfieldians on film during his career of over forty years. His studio was at 215 West Commercial Street.

Springfield was an important milling center for flour, cornmeal, and commercial feed. By 1942, eighteen mills, including the Springfield Flour Mills at 602 North National Avenue, employed three hundred forty-five men and had a yearly payroll of $375,000.

The Atlantic & Pacific and the St. Louis-San Francisco railroads supplied and carried to market the manufactured goods of several large businesses. They included the Springfield Wagon Factory, the Springfield Cotton Mills, the Springfield Woolen Mills, and the Queen City Mills. Queen City Mills produced one hundred fifty barrels of flour per day, most of which was shipped to eastern and southern markets. In 1880, livestock shipped out of Springfield included 3,040 head of fat cattle, 17,030 hogs, 5,100 sheep, and 532 mules and horses for a total value of $303,550. Springfield became the principal regional shipping point for other agricultural products as well, including cotton, wool, wheat, oats, tobacco, hides, poultry, dairy products, corn, potatoes and other vegetables.

The railroad and the growth it produced also led to greater ethnic diversity in Springfield's population. The first white settlers in southwest Missouri were primarily immigrants from Tennessee, Kentucky and North Carolina. It was written that "It is no rare thing to find some remote valley in the Ozark Center in which every inhabitant is descended from Tennessee stock." African Americans also were part of the population, originally brought in to work as slaves for the white settlers.

After the Civil War, however, the makeup of southwest Missouri began to change as people from a greater variety of state and ethnic backgrounds began moving into the area. The bulk of these new European settlers in the Ozarks were Germans emigrating either directly from Germany or coming from older cities such as St. Louis and Baltimore. Railroad companies advertised for settlers in Germany with the result that a number of German towns sprang up along the railroad routes.

German immigrants were notably successful as farmers but also made a significant impact on commerce in Springfield. They owned several large and successful dry goods and furniture stores, mills, and breweries. The immigrants maintained their ethnic identity through *Der Deutsch-Amerikanische Bund* (German-American League) and a meeting place called Germania Hall on Boonville Avenue. Many of them traded at the German-American Bank in Springfield.

**The Colonial Baking Company opened in 1929 at 828 East St. Louis Street, its current location. Its fleet of thirty-nine trucks served Springfield and the surrounding territory.**

**The Springfield Stockyards at 1605 East Olive Street provided a market for regionally produced beef and dairy cattle, hogs, goats, and sheep. This photograph was taken around 1930.**

**Below:**
**The Missouri Farmers' Association (M.F.A.) Milling Company sponsored a wartime display of garments and quilts made by the Women's Progressive Farmers Association. All the articles were made from M.F.A. flour and feed bags in 1942.**

28

Charles Heer came to the United States from Germany in the 1820s, settling first in St. Louis. After selling his successful business in Waterloo, Iowa, he came to Springfield in 1868 where he opened a dry goods store. Heer's Department Store, in business from 1869 until 1995, was family owned until the 1940s and was a pivotal business on the public square.

One of Heer's many departments sold the latest models of stoves and refrigerators in 1941.

Ben Lipman, shown with his sister Sonja Shechter, owned and operated Springfield's kosher market at 657 South Market Avenue. Their father, Jacob Lipman, was rabbi for the Congregation Share Zadek. Photograph courtesy of David Lipman.

A group of Swedish immigrants came on the Frisco Railroad to Greene County, and in 1886 this community organized the Swedish Lutheran Church.

Springfield's first Jewish resident, Victor Sommers, opened a dry goods store on Boonville Avenue in 1868, and within a few years other Jewish families, mostly German-born, arrived. By 1890 more than a dozen Jewish-owned businesses were flourishing on and around Springfield's public square as brothers, sisters and cousins joined families already established in the town.

Ramey's, Springfield's first supermarket, opened in the new Plaza Shopping Center at Sunshine Street and Glenstone Avenue in 1946.

African Americans, many of whom came to Springfield following the Civil War, also became active in the business community. They worked as dentists, morticians, blacksmiths and lawyers. At the time, Hardwick Brothers was the largest grocery store in the city. Walter "Duck" Majors built the first automobile in Springfield and had thirteen patents to his name including a taxicab meter and a hair dryer. He moved to St. Louis around 1907. J. H. Stemmons served on the public school board from 1894–1898. The first black public official, Alfred Adams who served as county coroner, was elected in 1878.

During the first two decades after the turn of the century, the economy became more diversified. Lead mining, brewing, carriage building, printing, lumber processing and iron working took their places in the manufacturing sector. The railroad continued in a dominant role providing both access to outside markets and employment for hundreds of citizens on the trains and in the machine shops. The completion of Highway 66 in 1926 gave Springfield a paved highway connection stretching from Chicago to Los Angeles and opened the way for tourism.

Yellow Bonnet was the signature label of the Springfield Grocer Company, founded in 1865. It remains as Springfield's oldest surviving business and is now one of the largest commercial food distributors in Southwest Missouri. Photograph courtesy of the Springfield Grocer Company.

Busy Bee Department Store, on Route 66, was on the southeast corner of College Street and Campbell Avenue. The popular store was owned and operated by Arthur Rosen who came to the United States in 1934 to escape Nazi terrorism.

The Great Depression brought economic privation in the region as it did to the rest of the United States in the 1930s. Demand for goods became so low that prices plummeted, yet many people could still barely afford to buy the necessities of life because they were out of work or their wages had been reduced.

Franklin Roosevelt's New Deal programs were perhaps the most visible manifestations of the depression in Springfield. The Public Works Administration (PWA) and later the Works Progress Administration (WPA) were federal agencies that funded massive public works projects. In Springfield, schools, parks, and public buildings were built by the PWA, including Dickerson Park Zoo, Silver Springs Park and the State Normal School's (now Southwest Missouri State University) McDonald Arena. The WPA also financed the rounding of curbs at intersections such as National Avenue and Walnut Street. The Reconstruction Finance Corporation (RFC), a federal relief agency that helped banks and corporations remain solvent, lent money to a number of Springfield charities in 1932.

**Union National Bank, at the southeast corner of the public square, was founded in 1899 by the McDaniel family. As seen around 1920, Dr. Weiner, dentist, and W. G. Gideon, lawyer, had offices above the bank. A new structure, taking up the entire southeast section of the square, opened in 1970. In 1974 the institution merged with Boatmen's Bancshares of St. Louis, and in 1997 Boatmen's was purchased by NationsBank.**

Hiland was one of a number of locally owned and operated dairies. Many area farmers specialized in dairy farming. Milk was processed in Springfield and shipped all over the country as butter, powdered milk, and frozen cream. In 1942 Springfield was described as "the hub of the cheese industry of the south."

Empire Bank opened for business in July of 1956 at 1800 South Glenstone Avenue and in 1959 became the first Springfield bank to offer extended hours. In 1980 Empire became a part of Central Bancompany.

Like the period after the Civil War in the 1870s, economic and population growth again experienced a spurt after World War II. The city changed from primarily an agricultural distribution center to an industrial city. In the 1950s the business community made an all out effort to attract light industry. During the next twenty-five years Lily Tulip Cup Corporation, Dayton Rubber Company, Royal Typewriter Company, Minnesota Mining and Manufacturing (3M), Zenith Radio Corporation, and R. T. French would establish plants here.

In recent years, the health and medical industry has come to dominate the economy centering on the so-called "medical mile" in south central Springfield. A number of locally owned businesses such as Conco Companies, Paul Mueller Company, Meeks Lumber, O'Reilly Auto Parts, Positronics, Springfield Remanufacturing, Bass Pro Shops and John Q. Hammons Industries and Hotels continue to provide economic stability and diversity. Tourism also stimulates many areas of the local economy. Bass Pro Shops is Missouri's number one attraction.

Springfield continues to move away from its agricultural roots and is experiencing steady growth in the medical, tourism, education, retail, and manufacturing industries as they respond to the needs of a growing population, employment and income.

**The Skelly station at the southwest corner of Elm Street and National Boulevard provided gasoline and full service for Springfield's growing number of privately owned automobiles, circa 1945.**

Mary Barnes and her husband Moses own and operate Vita-Erb, manufacturing cosmetics for a nationwide clientele. The Small Business Administration honored Barnes in 1991 as the Women in Business Advocate of the Year for the four-state region.

**Above:**
The Leong family owns and operates Leong's Tea House, Springfield's first Chinese restaurant, which opened on West Sunshine Street in 1963.

The Lily Tulip Cup Corporation was one of the first major manufacturing plants built in Springfield, opening its doors in June of 1952. Executives of the company were attracted by the town's friendliness and fair labor practices.

Passengers who arrived at the Frisco Railroad depot in 1922 found transportation available to their final destination from the Pickwick Baggage and Taxicab Company. In the heyday of railroad travel the company kept this fleet of vehicles ready at the depot.

# 4

# The Crossroads Come Alive

From notices posted on trees to those posted on the Internet and from horses with wagons to engines with horse power, the development of modern transportation and communication has been a key factor in the growth of Springfield.

Horses or mules served as transportation for the early settlers for riding and pulling wagons and carriages. The first major transportation link outside the city came with the start of stagecoach service in 1858 by Butterfield Overland Mail.

The coming of the "iron horse" to this area in 1870 meant a new means of travel and communication as well as a new way of shipping and receiving for business and industry. Railroads serving the city included the Atlantic & Pacific, the Gulf, the St. Louis-San Francisco (Frisco) and the Missouri Pacific. The railroad played an important part in the community for over a century. As other means of transportation became more available, the railroad phased out passenger service. The last passenger train arrived in Springfield from St. Louis in May of 1967.

Because horse power was so important to the community, the veterinarian was much in demand before the turn of the century as this shot of Dr. Love's Veterinary Ambulance (with large patient) shows.

Above:
The Butterfield Overland Mail first arrived in Springfield in 1858 carrying passengers and mail from Tipton, Missouri to the West Coast. It opened up for the city a vital link with the rest of the nation. This photograph shows a reenactment of the arrival of the stage in connection with the centennial of the event.

The Atlantic & Pacific Railroad laid its tracks to the north of the town of Springfield when it arrived in 1870. As a result, the town of North Springfield sprang up along the tracks, and the railroad depot was built at Benton Avenue and Commercial Street.

Walter L. "Duck" Majors is pictured at the wheel of an automobile he built. (Photograph Courtesy of Katherine Lederer)

Street cars, which first appeared in 1881, provided public transportation service to residents for over fifty years. The city was one of the first in the nation to install electric trolleys in 1885.

The development of the gasoline engine and the automobile brought great individual freedom of movement to residents. The first privately owned automobile arrived in Springfield in 1905 when the population was approximately twenty-four thousand. Walter "Duck" Majors built the first automobile in Springfield in the early 1900s. At that time his red car was called the "Walter Majors machine." Today, there are approximately 200,000 vehicles registered in the city. Commercial bus transportation, both intra- and inter-city, also came to Springfield.

Thanks to motorized vehicles, good roads, and a geographical location in the center of the country, Springfield soon became a transportation hub and a regional center for business and industry. The completion of Highway 66 in 1926 allowed for easier and increased travel in and out of Springfield.

In the early 1920s Springfieldians took to the skies. Invention of the airplane brought another vital, and quicker, link with the world. First flights in the early 1920s were made from a private airfield on Dollison Avenue south of Phelps Grove Park. These early beginnings laid the foundation for the development of a modern regional airport, Springfield-Branson Regional Airport located at 5000 West Kearney Street, which provides a portal to the rest of the world.

When the railroad line was extended to the southeast, a second terminal was built at 604 West Mill Street in downtown Springfield and used until 1967 when passenger service was discontinued. This depot housed the very popular Harvey House restaurant.

Below:
The steam engine, long a familiar sight on the railroad lines through the city, gradually gave way to diesel-powered engines. The Frisco Railroad gave way to the Burlington Northern Railroad after consolidation in 1980. Photograph courtesy of the Frisco Railroad Museum.

The Frisco Railroad diesel shops, which opened in the northwest part of the city in 1909, made the Frisco Springfield's largest employer through World War II. The shops were closed by Burlington Northern in 1996.

Morgan
Photo

The center of much of the early railroad activity in Springfield was this large roundhouse located on Commercial Street in North Springfield.

The earliest streetcars, first appearing in 1881, were mule-drawn vehicles which connected the public square with Commercial Street. They were replaced by electric cars in 1885. Springfieldians could board a streetcar on the public square; this loading area is near where Boonville Avenue enters the square. From there they could go as far north as Doling Park and as far east as Springfield Normal School on Pickwick Avenue.

**Above:**
Excited patrons packed the streetcars for a free ride on their last day of use — August 30, 1937.

**Left:**
Buses such as this Springfield Traction Company vehicle became the prevailing means of public transportation in the 1930s as streetcar service was phased out.

Communication, in the early days, was often limited to word-of-mouth. Information in writing was expanded with the introduction of the first post office in 1834. In 1860, lines of communication were extended even further when a telegraph line running from Jefferson City to Fort Smith, Arkansas came through the city. It was later joined during the Civil War by a line to St. Louis.

Newspapers have been a communication link since the city's first paper, the *Ozarks Standard*, appeared in 1837. Several papers have come and gone during the intervening years or have been consolidated to form the present-day *Springfield News-Leader*. The printed word has expanded over the years to include such local publications as *Springfield!* magazine and *Springfield Business Journal*.

Springfield druggist Edward Woelk had the first telephone in Missouri used for business and opened an exchange in his home in 1878. Today there are fifty-eight exchanges (including those used for residential, cellular, and pager services) keeping residents connected.

Radio, the next marvel of technology, first made its appearance in the city in the form of experimental station WAIA. It operated in the Heer's store from 1922 to 1925. Development of commercial radio began several years later. There are now twenty-one AM and FM stations.

Television came to Springfield in 1953 and opened the world even more for Springfieldians. Today, counting new low-power stations, there are seven television stations. In addition, thousands of people now have increased viewing opportunities available to them through cable television. The broadcasting stations and new satellite technology have allowed in-home viewing of events around the globe as they happen.

A newspaper business has been housed in this plant on Boonville Avenue since 1947 when a fire destroyed the previous building. The *Springfield News-Leader*, a division of Gannett Co., operates out of this building today.

In 1942 Springfield voters approved the construction of a new airport northwest of the city. This wooden structure served as the city's front door until 1963.

As flying became more popular in the 1920s, McCluer Airfield was developed east of town. It was taken over by the city in 1928 and served as the city's airport until the early 1940s. It is still in operation as the privately owned Downtown Airport at 2546 East Division.

As the year 2000 rapidly approaches, even more individualized contacts throughout the world are being made possible by the ever-expanding technology of the Internet. Several community agencies came together in 1994 to provide Springfieldians access to the latest in electronic communications. They started Ozarks Regional Informational Online Network (ORION) which allows residents to communicate through the Internet. More opportunities are quickly becoming available through the use of digital switching offices and fiber optic technology which today are expanding throughout the city.

All of the improvements in transportation and communication have resulted in making the citizens of Springfield truly citizens of the world.

Since it came on the scene in 1932, radio has provided an important means of communication. In addition to keeping people informed through news broadcasts, the medium has given residents a chance to be heard on such programs as "Montage" during the 1970s on KGBX. Jerry Higley was the radio personality.

In the early days of telephone, the main telephone switchboard, shown here in 1926, was what kept the community connected. In today's modern world computers and electronic switching apparatus handle the job.

Shortly after it went on the air in 1953, the city's first television station, KTTS, started televising events in the schools on "Television Classroom," a program which lasted for a quarter of a century. (KTTS is now KOLR.) Photograph courtesy of Springfield Public Schools.

Improvements in equipment soon provided television station KYTV an opportunity to do remote broadcasts or tape events as they happened for immediate playback. Today, the remote taping trucks have been replaced with equipment that uses satellite uplinks or microwave technology to allow live coverage just about anywhere in the world. Photograph courtesy of Richard Grosenbaugh.

Satellite technology provides instantaneous communications around the globe. That technology is used extensively by TCI of Springfield which came to the city in 1980 and now provides more than sixty channels of information and entertainment. The same satellite technology can send information directly to individual homes. Photograph courtesy of Richard Grosenbaugh.

The first public senior high school, Springfield High School, in 1894 was located at Jefferson Avenue and Center (now Central) Street. It is now named Central High School.

# 5

## Learning To Make Life Better

"It is more than likely that none of us recognize what this work of education is, fully and really what it is to accomplish; but one thing is certain, that without it we may be savages, and with it we may aspire to be angels; that education is power, and that ignorance is weakness; that the man or woman who expects to get the most out of life must be educated, must have his faculties developed, trained, drawn out and made strong. We do not want simply the few to be educated, but the many - *all.*"

1887 Public Schools Annual Report
Jonathan Fairbanks, Superintendent

The arrival of Joseph Rountree in 1831 resulted in the establishment of the first school in Springfield. This one room log cabin school was located on what is now Mount Vernon Street. A new schoolhouse was built a year later on the northwest corner of what is now Main Avenue and College Street. This new school had "a loose plank floor, a door shutter, and a mud and stick chimney." The schoolhouse was later used by First Christian Church.

Private schools continued in these early years, and in 1842 John Stephens took subscriptions for Springfield's first academy: Springfield Academy, also known as Stephen Academy, located on Short Benton Avenue, just north of St. Louis Street. Among the pupils at Stephens Academy was Colonel S. H. "Pony" Boyd who grew up to be one of Springfield's most picturesque and notable politicians. There were other private colleges prior to the Civil War, most notably, Carlton College, established by clergyman Charles Carlton and located at College Street near Main Avenue.

Public schools were established in Springfield in September of 1867 with the first enrollment totaling two hundred four in elementary, sixty-eight in high school and forty-eight in the "Colored" School. The first school term began in September and lasted seven and a half months. Public school classes met in rented facilities until Central School was built in 1871 at Olive Street and Jefferson Avenue to house all grades. Several ward schools followed, and the community's first building specifically designed for high school students was built at the corner of Jefferson Avenue and Center (now Central) Street in 1893. With several additions, Springfield High School served as the district's only high school until 1954 and continues to serve students today, now as Central High School which is on the National Register of Historic Places.

The Springfield Academy, also known as Stephens Academy, was housed in this two-story building on Short Benton Avenue, one block north of St. Louis Street. A University Club plaque marks the site where the building once stood.

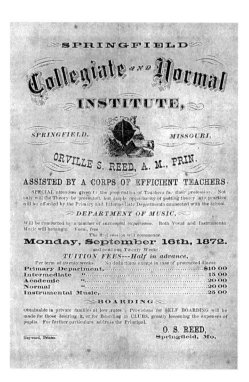

An 1872 flyer from the private Collegiate and Normal Institute offered curriculum to prepare teachers for their profession.

Joseph Rountree was the first school teacher in Springfield. He was born in 1782, the youngest of a large family, and died at the age of ninety-two in 1874. He and his wife, Nancy Nichols, had ten children.

Springfield's first public school building, Central School (shown circa 1871), was located at Olive Street and Jefferson Avenue. This building was sold in 1910, and the Landmark Building, first known as the Frisco Building, now stands on this site.

CENTRAL SCHOOL BUILDING, SPRINGFIELD, MO.

Jonathan Fairbanks, Superintendent of the Public Schools from 1875 to 1912, is shown standing near his home on North Sherman Avenue in the early 1900s. The house was razed in 1997.

Enrollment in the public schools was steady until the 1950s and 1960s when many new buildings were needed to handle an enrollment which peaked at close to twenty-five thousand. Many of the present-day school buildings were built in the 1950s and 1960s. There are now five high schools, nine middle schools, and thirty-nine elementary schools. Current enrollment for the Springfield Public Schools totals 24,876.

When Springfield began its public school system in 1867, African American students met in a Methodist Church. In 1872 the public "Colored" School opened between Benton Avenue and Washington Avenue, south of what is Burnham Hall on Drury College campus. Renamed and relocated in 1883 from Drury's campus to Center Street (now Central) and Washington Avenue, Lincoln School graduated its first three members in 1888. In 1931 a new Lincoln School was built at Central Street and Sherman Avenue. This was the first school in Missouri (of four total) built by the Julius Rosenwald Foundation, an organization dedicated to improving black education in southern and border states. It still stands on the campus of Ozarks Technical Community College at 815 Sherman Avenue and is on the National Register of Historic Places.

Springfield Schools remained segregated until the U.S. Supreme Court decision in *Brown v. Board of Education* in 1954. The district, under the direction of Superintendent Willard Graff, was one of the first in the nation to successfully integrate after the Brown decision. The young girl who lent her name to the historic desegregation case, Linda Brown, was graduated from Central High School in 1961, having moved here from Kansas.

The first Lincoln School, built for African American students, was located at the southeast corner of Central Street and Washington Avenue. This property was purchased by Drury College in the 1970s and razed to create space for a parking lot.

Private and parochial elementary and secondary schools have also played an important role in the education of Springfield students. The Catholic Loretto Academy began in 1878 at Campbell Avenue and Pine (now Tampa) Street. The Catholic churches have offered an education system since 1892 when St. Joseph's School was started in a stable on the Heer property. The school later moved into a new building on Scott Street in 1908. Today the Catholic school system offers educational programs for more than thirteen hundred students, preschool through high school age, in five school buildings. In addition to the Catholic School System, Springfield now has Lutheran schools, Christian schools, and Greenwood Laboratory School.

This is the 1944 graduating class from the new Lincoln School located at Central Street and Sherman Avenue. *First row left to right:* Mary Dean, Alma Logan, Marion Weaver, Charlene Fulbright, Mildred Pike, Sarah Jackson, Mary Anna Graham, Florence Parks. *Second Row:* Alfred Culp, Howard Green, Betty Denton, Lester Dukes, Milton Hanks, Carrena Davis, Howell Lewis, and Class Sponsor, Zanthia Cooper. The building is now on the National Register of Historic Places and serves as the administration building for Ozarks Technical Community College.

The Class of 1913 at Boyd School is shown with the school's namesake, Mary Boyd, sitting in the center. The school is located at Washington Avenue and Lynn Street and was built in 1908. Mary Boyd opened a private school during the Civil War, and in 1867 she began teaching in the first Springfield public school, Central School, at Olive Street and Jefferson Avenue. She taught in the same classroom until her retirement in 1908. To honor her dedication, a new school was named after her. Mary Boyd died in 1918 at the age of eighty-three.

A class of students posed in front of Douglass School, the Springfield school system's elementary school for African American students, circa 1900. Douglass was built in 1892 at 835 South Main Avenue. It was closed in 1932 and later razed.

Many Springfield girls attended school at St. de Chantal Academy, opened by the Sisters of the Visitation in 1906. It closed its doors to students in 1964. The house was built before the turn of the century as a home for the O'Day family and called Elfindale. After changing owners several times, the property is now owned by the Cornerstone Church, and an independently operated bed and breakfast is housed in the mansion.

Construction of the drive in front of the old Greenwood School building on Southwest Missouri State Teachers College campus, circa 1920. Carrington Hall is in the background.

This photograph was entitled "The Indian Boys at Fairbanks Hall 1894-95." Photograph courtesy of Drury College Archives.

Stone Chapel on the Drury College Campus, built in 1883, is on the National Register of Historic Places.

Pictured is the Drury College Class of 1903. *First row left to right:* Maude Little, Charlie Orr, Vera Brereton, Professor Finkel's daughter, and Ed Hall. *Second Row:* Emery Lowe, Mamie Brockman, Effie Sterrett, Ellen Craig, Evelyn Mucke, Grace Williams, and Alice Jane Bennett. *Third row:* Grant Johnson, Bertha Booth, and George Sam Will.

Higher education as we know it today began with Springfield College in 1873. This liberal arts college, now known as Drury College, was started by the Congregational Church. The original class of 1873 enrolled thirty-nine students of which seven were Native Americans, five men and two women. Today Drury enrolls 3,524 undergraduates and graduates.

The local state university began as the privately owned Springfield Normal School, founded in 1894 at Pickwick Avenue and Cherry Street. This institution had the distinction of playing the first night football game west of the Mississippi River in 1904. The game was against the Cherokee Indians, from Tahlequah, Indian Territory. Springfield Normal won the game.

After the State of Missouri approved establishment of a normal school in 1905, the building at Pickwick Avenue and Cherry Street housed State Normal until a new campus was started in its present location on South National Avenue in 1906 with the construction of the current administration building, Carrington Hall, formerly Academic Hall. During that first year State Normal had 543 students. In 1919 the school's name was changed to Southwest Missouri State Teachers College and had a fall enrollment of 499 students. By 1945, "Teachers" was removed from its name, and in 1972 its designation was further upgraded to that of a university, representing the broad range of educational opportunities it offered. Today Southwest Missouri State University enrolls 16,364 graduate and undergraduate students.

Several other institutions of higher education operated by religious denominations add to the educational climate of the community. The oldest of these is Central Bible College (formerly Institute) formed in 1922 when the Commercial Club of Springfield gave fifteen acres to the Assemblies of God. The Assemblies of God founded Evangel College in 1955, a liberal arts college housed on the former O'Reilly Army Hospital grounds. Current enrollment at Evangel is 1,574. Baptist Bible College was opened in 1950 by the Baptist Bible Fellowship to train young people for religious work. Today the institution enrolls almost nine hundred students.

Throughout the years other types of institutions have served to educate young men and women for various careers. Queen City Business College was the first business school to open in 1892. Draughon Business College followed shortly thereafter, opening in 1904. These schools offered courses in civil service, comptometry, typewriting, bookkeeping, stenography, machine accounting, accountancy, stenotypy and salesmanship. Springfield now has two business schools, Vatterott College, originally Draughon Business College, and Springfield College, originally Springfield Business School which was established in 1910. Ozarks Technical Community College (which grew out of Graff Vocational-Technical School) began in 1990 as the region's comprehensive community college emphasizing job-skill training programs supplemented by a wide variety of general education courses. This school enrolls twelve thousand students in its high school technical, customized training and college credit programs.

Over the years the educational opportunities have evolved to meet the ever-changing needs of society and the Springfield community.

**This building at Pickwick Avenue and Cherry Street housed the Springfield Normal School until State Normal was formed in 1905. Although on the outskirts of town, it was made accessible by a new streetcar line. The building was razed in 1916.**

A bird's-eye view shows Southwest Missouri State Teachers College, now Southwest Missouri State University, circa 1950. The campus was surrounded by residential housing which has been removed to make way for university expansion.

Draughon Business College was opened in 1904 at 218 West Walnut Street and served the community until 1991 when it closed at 1258 East Trafficway. This photograph shows a 1920s student-operated store which was part of the business training program.

Early Ozark baptisms were often performed in local rivers and streams, emulating Jesus' baptism in the River Jordan.

# 6

# Keeping the Faith

Springfield has long been known as a city of churches, and within its houses of religion is woven much of the city's history. Religion played a vital role in the lives of nineteenth-century and twentieth-century Americans, and Springfield was no exception.

The Rev. James Slavens preached the first sermon here in 1831, starting a congregation of the Methodist Episcopal Church. By 1833 this group had built an eighteen-by-twenty-foot log meeting house near the Fairbanks Spring at a cost of eighteen dollars; the Cumberland Presbyterians also met in the building for a brief time. The spring today is in Silver Springs Park on North National Avenue between Scott and Division streets. Rev. Slavens' saddle-bags are preserved at St. Paul United Methodist Church at 413 East Walnut.

Other denominations also founded congregations in these early years. First Christian Church, First Cumberland and Calvary Presbyterian churches, and First Baptist Church were among those who built houses of worship in the 1840s and 1850s.

Church attendance was difficult during the Civil War. Many congregations were divided over the issue of slavery, and the disruption of the war itself closed down most churches. Calvary Presbyterian was the only Springfield church that held services during the Civil War. The Reverend Frederick Wines, appointed Union military chaplain for Springfield, ministered to the community as well. Wines conducted services at Calvary Presbyterian, on South Jefferson Avenue near Elm Street, taught Sunday School for all ages, and acquired books for the church from friends in New Jersey.

When the war was over a number of African American congregations sprang up for newly freed slaves, including Gibson Chapel and Washington Avenue Baptist Church. Many other churches renewed their building programs. Calvary Presbyterian Church built a new sanctuary in 1882 on the John S. Phelps lot at the northwest corner of St. Louis Street and Benton Avenue, the present site of Mercantile Bank. First Cumberland Presbyterian Church, established in 1849, constructed a new building at Jefferson Avenue and Olive Street after the war. The two Presbyterian churches merged in 1930 with the new name of First and Calvary in a new building at Cherry Street and Dollison Avenue, now John Q. Hammons Parkway.

Other churches, including First Christian, South Street Christian, First Baptist and Grace Methodist built new and larger sanctuaries in the center city area before the turn of the century. First Congregational Church, built in 1872 at Jefferson Avenue and Locust Street, served many in North Springfield, including professors and their families from Drury College which was founded by the Congregational Church in 1873.

**Frederick Wines, a graduate of Princeton Theological Seminary, was the pastor of the Calvary Presbyterian congregation as well as a post chaplain of the Union Army. The photograph was taken in Springfield during the Civil War.**

**After the Civil War, Calvary Presbyterian Church built a newer and larger building to house their growing congregation located on the northwest corner of St. Louis Street and Benton Avenue. This building was dedicated March 19, 1882. It is now the site of Mercantile Bank.**

Temple Israel, built in 1930 by the United Hebrew Congregations, was at the corner of Belmont Street and Kickapoo Avenue. The congregations moved in 1996 to a new location south of Springfield.

Bentley Chapel, at the southeast corner of South Avenue and Pershing Street, was a Methodist Episcopal church dedicated in May of 1870.

The congregation of Bentley Chapel changed their name to Grace Methodist Episcopal Church and built a new sanctuary which was completed in 1895 on the site at South Avenue and Pershing Street. Grace United Methodist has occupied its current location at 600 South Jefferson Avenue since 1923.

Christ Episcopal Church, built in 1870, is the city's oldest original church building. Located at the northeast corner of Walnut Street and Kimbrough Avenue, it is on the National Register of Historic Places.

Springfield's first Roman Catholic church, Immaculate Conception, came into being in 1868 at North Campbell Avenue and Tampa Street. The oldest original Catholic building is Sacred Heart Church, built at 1609 North Summit Avenue, primarily for Irish parishioners. This 1882 building was rebuilt on the original site in 1884 following a tornado. St. Joseph's Catholic Church, still in its historic 1904 building at Campbell Avenue and Scott Street, was founded in 1892 as a parish church for German-speaking Catholics.

Food is packed at the Ozarks Food Harvest, an agency of the Council of Churches of the Ozarks, for distribution to those in need.

Other German-Americans attended St. John's Evangelical Church at Main Avenue and Scott Street in North Springfield and Evangelical Lutheran Trinity Church located at Jefferson Avenue and Elm Street.

Springfield's Jewish residents organized a worshiping congregation in 1893. Temple Israel, affiliated with American Reformed Judaism, met in rented space until their own building opened at Lombard Street and Kickapoo Avenue in 1930. A group of Orthodox Jews shared the building and rabbi with Temple Israel. The United Hebrew Congregations moved to a new location in 1996, now meeting two miles south of Springfield on Farm Road 193.

A major addition to Springfield's religious life came in 1918 when the Assemblies of God, the world's largest Pentecostal denomination, relocated its international headquarters in the city. First located at Lyon Avenue and Pacific Street, the Assemblies of God built a new and much larger headquarters at Boonville Avenue and Division Street, former site of White City Park, where the Assemblies still stand. Springfield also serves as headquarters for the independent Baptist group, Baptist Bible Fellowship, organized in 1950.

Before the Second World War much of the benevolence work in Springfield was handled by the American Red Cross and the Salvation Army. Most churches carried out their mission by preaching the word. By the 1960s, however, churches began to practice the concept of benevolence along with evangelism. The founding of the Council of Churches of the Ozarks started in 1967 a new era of ecumenical cooperation.

Many of Springfield's churches support the Council of Churches of the Ozarks with money and service to the Council's many charitable programs. These programs include the emergency food and clothing pantry Crosslines, Ozarks Food Harvest food bank and Sigma House, a place where low-income men and women can receive residential treatment for drug and alcohol addiction.

St. Agnes Catholic Church began in 1908 in a newly established parish in what was then south Springfield. It remains at its original location at Cherry Street and Jefferson Avenue and became a cathedral in 1956.

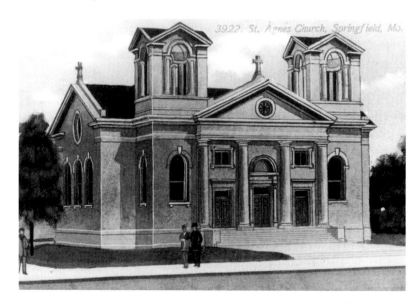

Organized in 1867, Washington Avenue Baptist Church is the mother church of several other congregations in the Southwest Baptist Convention. The current building at 729 North Washington Avenue is a historic site.

The 1945 confirmation class posed outside of Sacred Heart Catholic Church located at 1609 North Summit Avenue. After a tornado destroyed the building, another church was built on the site and was completed around 1884. It is the oldest continuously occupied Catholic church southwest of Rolla, Missouri.

Other organizations also attempt to meet the needs of the increasing number of disadvantaged and homeless. The Springfield-Cape Girardeau Diocese of the Roman Catholic Church helps to underwrite work of The Kitchen/Missouri Hotel homeless shelter and soup kitchen, and the Springfield Victory Mission is funded by private donations. Local Baptists support Grand Oaks Mission.

Today there are over two hundred churches in the Queen City, still the city of churches.

First Baptist Church, at 457 South Avenue, is shown after the last service in its second building on September 2, 1951. The church was founded by Reverend Braxton McCord Roberts in 1852 as a branch of the Liberty Baptist Church.

The International Headquarters of the Assemblies of God, at 1445 Boonville Avenue, contains the Gospel Publishing House, a large office complex, and a distribution center. The Theological Seminary has recently moved into a new facility on the campus of Evangel College.

Christ Episcopal Church is located at the northeast corner of Walnut Street and Kimbrough Avenue and is pictured circa 1920. It is the oldest original church building in Springfield, built in 1870.

**A group of sixty-seven Red Cross volunteers posed outside of the War Dads' Canteen at the Frisco Depot during World War II.**

# Helping Hands

Many services for those who need help have been provided in Springfield through governmental and private organizations throughout the years. Formed as the Community Chest, the United Way continues to support health, community betterment, and youth-serving organizations. There are also a number of organizations devoted to conquering specific health problems and helping those in financial need.

The women's club movement was begun shortly after the Civil War when community betterment problems needed to be solved. Founding clubs on the principle of service, women's efforts have advanced education and civic improvement.

These important factors of the city's history relied heavily upon a strong spirit of volunteerism and philanthropy. Springfieldians have demonstrated their willingness to help when called upon to serve.

**Left:**
James Hervey Slavens, a minister and doctor, married Louisa Amanda Rountree, daughter of pioneer and teacher Joseph Rountree.

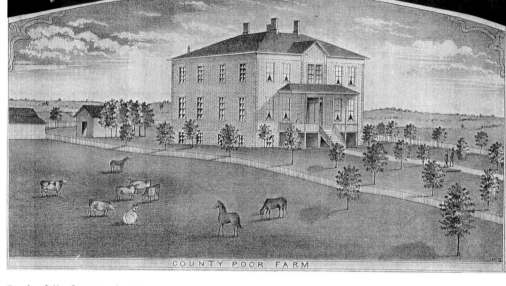

In the fall of 1855, the Greene County Court authorized a county almshouse or poor farm for the care of the sick, insane, and poor. A property tax was levied to purchase two hundred acres, construct a building, and improve the farm. In 1873 a new building (pictured here) was built on eighty acres just outside the eastern city limits. This engraving was reprinted from the 1876 *Greene County Historical Atlas.*

**Left:**
Dr. Christopher Columbus Clements married Albina (Binnie) Parrish who founded the Binnie Clements Guild at First and Calvary Presbyterian Church.

Springfield has long been known for the quality of its medical centers, and in the early days the town did not lack for physicians. The practice of medicine was rudimentary by today's standards, but the health care was very likely typical for its time.

The first physician was probably Dr. Edward Rodgers, who came from Tennessee in 1831, stayed a few years, and moved to Texas. Dr. Cornelius Terrell, a practicing physician who was also active in politics, was appointed the second county clerk in 1834.

Dr. Thomas Jefferson Bailey moved to Springfield around 1835 to 1837. He had a successful practice and was active in civic affairs and business, becoming vice-president of a savings bank in 1867. The monument at the Springfield National Cemetery, dedicated to the memory of the Federal soldiers who died at the Battle of Wilson's Creek, was paid for by Dr. Bailey.

James Hervey Slavens, a Methodist circuit rider, preached Springfield's first religious service in 1831. He began studying medicine with Dr. Bailey, helping with the large practice until about 1840 when he established his own practice.

Dr. C. C. Clements was born in Tennessee, served as a surgeon in the Union army, and came to Springfield in 1867. He helped organize the Springfield Medical Society and was its president for several years. He was president of the Board of Health at various times and president of the Springfield Board of Pension Examiners.

William M. Smith moved to Springfield in 1888 with his wife and four children. Dr. Smith was president of the Greene County Medical Society for a term, a member of the Southwest Missouri Medical Society, the Missouri State Medical and American Medical Associations, and on the executive board of Burge Hospital. Their sons graduated from Beaumont Medical College in St. Louis; Wells Ferrin Smith in 1898 and Wilbur Smith in 1901.

Dr. Wilbur Smith and Dr. Wallis Smith (no relation) formed the first "partnership for the practice of medicine" in 1922. Dr. Robert Glynn and Dr. Guy Callaway were added in 1924. Their practice moved between the Holland and Smith buildings from 1922 to 1955. With the death of Dr. Wilbur Smith in 1934, the Smith-Glynn-Callaway Clinic added Dr. Daniel Yancey, the first certified orthopedist in the area, and two years later, Dr. Durward Hall. Continuing to add services and new doctors, they built their own facility at 1211 South Glenstone Avenue in 1955. The clinic continued to expand, and a new, larger building was erected at 3231 South National Avenue in 1985 as part of the "medical mile." It was renamed the Springfield Clinic with its recent sale to St. John's Hospital.

By 1890 Springfield had a population of more than twenty-one thousand and needed a hospital. Dr. J. E. Tefft and the Ladies Hospital Aid Society brought the Sisters of Mercy to Springfield in 1891. St. John's Hospital was established in a two-story brick residence at Washington Avenue and Chestnut Street. In 1906, St. John's moved into a new structure at Main Avenue and Nichols Street. This building was enlarged and remodeled many times until 1952 when a new facility was built at 1235 East Cherokee Street, the hospital's present location. Now a regional medical center, St. John's is one of the largest in the Midwest.

Ellen Burge donated land and a large home at 1325 North Jefferson Avenue in 1906 for a medical facility. The first brick unit of Burge Deaconess Hospital was built to the south in 1908. A bequest allowed the construction of the John Howard Nixon Memorial Wing in 1932. In 1943 the Burge School of Nursing affiliated with Drury College. In 1949 under the leadership of businessman Lester E. Cox, extensive expansion began which included the City Hospital. At his death in 1968, his son Lester L. (Bud) Cox carried on the expansion. In 1969 the name was changed to Lester E. Cox Medical Center. Cox Hospital completed Primrose Place, a nursing home, at National Avenue and Primrose Street in 1984 in south Springfield. This began development of the so-called medical mile which soon included the new Cox South Hospital.

The Springfield Negro Clinic, later called the Community Hospital, was opened at 914 East Calhoun Street by 1921 and in operation until 1950. Kiddie Cove Day Care Center is now on the site.

A United States Medical Center for Federal Prisoners was dedicated at 1900 West Sunshine Street in 1932 and has treated hundreds of prisoners, including several well-known and notorious criminals: the Bird Man of Alcatraz, John Gotti, Larry Flynt, Sheik Omar Abdel Rahman, and Leonard Peltier.

**Dr. William McCullough Smith, a Civil War veteran, is shown at his desk circa 1900.**

This 1910 snapshot shows the second St. John's Hospital which was built in 1906 at the northwest corner of Main Avenue and Nichols Street. The original building and its addition are now occupied by Franciscan Villa.

In 1912, realizing that nurses were not only caregivers for sick individuals but an essential part of the public health campaign, the Springfield Visiting Nurse Association was started. Nurses educated families about cleanliness, nutrition, and self-care. Dentists, oculists, and specialists volunteered to provide their services through the association, and in 1914 the Springfield Board of Education appointed the first school nurse.

There have been numerous other agencies providing health and welfare services including churches, the American Red Cross, the Salvation Army, Camp Fire Boys and Girls, Y.M.C.A., Y.W.C.A., Boys and Girls Clubs, Ozarks Fighting Back, civic clubs, and women's organizations to name a few. Without volunteers such organizations would not be able to function. The "helping hands" of these volunteers are in the true spirit of Springfield and have served the area throughout its history.

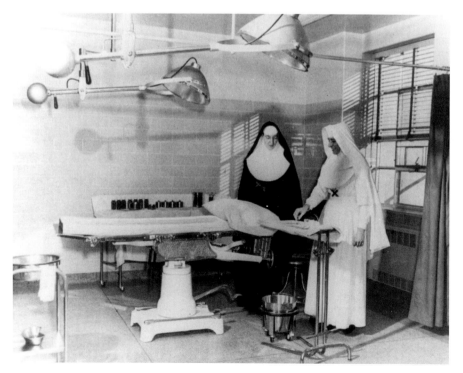

Under the leadership of the Sisters of Mercy, St. John's Hospital continued to grow. Shown in a 1953 photograph in their new hospital at 1235 South Cherokee Street are Sr. Mary Bertrand Dailey, RSM, administrator, and Sr. Mary Kathleen Cern, RSM.

In 1908 Burge Deaconess Hospital built a brick building, and the home at the right, originally used as the hospital, became a home and school for the nurses.

Ellen Starks Burge was born in 1843, came to Springfield with her family in 1860, and was married to George Burge in 1865. She was active in the Ladies Home Missionary Society of the Methodist Episcopal church, who were instrumental in supporting the hospital until her death in 1922. This engraving was reprinted from Fairbanks and Tuck, *Past and Present of Greene County, Missouri.*

In 1949 under the leadership of business-man Lester E. Cox, extensive expansion began at Burge Hospital which eventually became Lester E. Cox Medical Center.

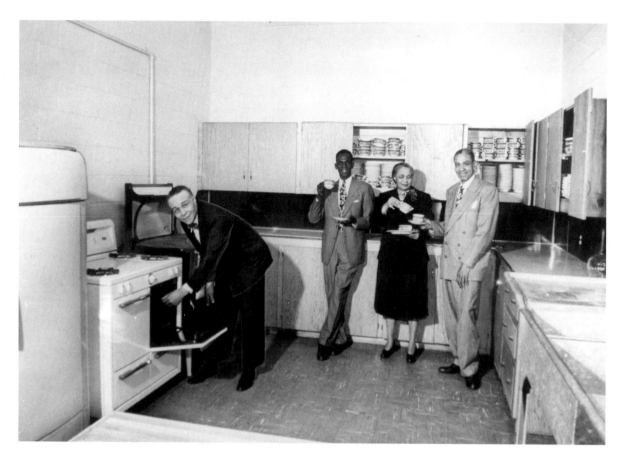

The Springfield Negro Community Youth Center and Norval Stafford American Legion Post was built in 1954 at 618 North Benton Avenue and served as an activity center for African American youths and Legion members in segregated Springfield. Four of the founders are shown in the kitchen at its opening. They are *(left to right)* E. C. Curtis, Thomas Darton, Mrs. E. C. Curtis, and Leslie Gipson. In 1995 the center was rebuilt and enlarged on the same site.

Arah Coleman, shown in this circa 1880 photograph, was employed as a nurse for the Dr. Horatio Parrish family.

The Frisco Railroad operated its own hospital for employees at Broadway Avenue and Atlantic Street from 1899 until 1922. The hospital was supported by a fifty cent per month assessment of each Frisco employee who made fifty dollars or more a month, or thirty-five cents for those who made less. Any employee who had an injury on the job could be treated there without charge for a year.

Springfield Hospital opened for patients at 448-450 South Market Avenue on January 1, 1905. The growth of the hospital was so rapid that additions were made twice by 1908, and an annex was built in 1913. Growth continued as it became Springfield Baptist Hospital, then Park Central Hospital and now Lakeland Regional Hospital.

Springfield Hospital School of Nursing had a two-year program and graduated its first class of nurses in May, 1907. The class pictured here, if not the first, was a very early one.

Dr. Carlie Souter Smith was one of the earliest female medical doctors in Springfield and wife of Dr. Wallis Smith. She was an eye, ear, nose, and throat specialist from 1915 until her retirement in 1955. In 1953 Smith became the first woman to be elected to city council, serving for fourteen years. She was a member of the Drury College Board of Trustees, and Drury's Smith Hall was named in her honor.

Below:
Members of the nation-wide literary club, Friends in Council, are shown in this photograph taken in the winter of 1897–98. The local group was established in 1883 and joined the Federation of Women's Clubs in 1892 and the Missouri State Federation at its inception in 1896. Many of the members were active on committees such as the one which managed the Children's Home and in other philanthropic activities.

During the Centenary Missionary movement in 1919, the Missionary Society of St. Paul Methodist Church established the Centenary Training Home for orphan girls between the ages of eight and sixteen, located at 1600 West Phelps Street. The girls attended public schools, learned domestic work, and received religious instruction. This photograph was taken in 1935.

The Hopewells, founded in 1902, were probably best known for their "Milk Fund" which provided milk to needy families with children. With home deliveries no longer being made, the Milk Fund is now channeled through Crosslines. The old-fashioned milk can being held by Frances Ferguson was one of several placed in stores during the 1920s and 1930s to collect donations toward the fund. Also shown in the 1968 photograph are *(seated left to right)* Mary Eckert and Dala Sawyer. Standing are Nancy Farthing and Mary Luster.

In this 1861 sketch from *Harper's Weekly*, the newly completed Greene County Courthouse on the northwest corner of the public square is on the extreme right. The remains of the older, red brick courthouse is in the center. A demented prisoner in the old courthouse set fire to the building. The new courthouse served as a hospital during and after the Battle of Wilson's Creek. Illustration by Alexander Simplot.

# 8

# Serving Our Nation

Since its founding in 1830, the growing town of Springfield had been spared the menace of war, but the absence of armed conflict was interrupted first by the 1846 war with Mexico and then periodically throughout its history. War not only affects the men and women who wear the uniform but also those who remain behind and provide civilian support.

In 1846, one hundred ten men from Springfield, Company G, Third Missouri Mounted Volunteers traveled to Mexico to represent their country in the Mexican War. Only one-half of the company returned.

Springfield felt the impact of the Civil War early on as its second major battle was fought a few miles south of town at Wilson's Creek on August 10, 1861. General Nathaniel Lyon was the first Union general to die in battle. From that point on until the last occupying soldier left Springfield in 1865, the town was alternately occupied by Union or Confederate soldiers. It became a large military depot with four forts constructed at strategic locations throughout the town. One of the forts provided refuge for civilians while Fort No. 4, located on the east side of South Street just north of Mount Vernon Avenue, bore the brunt of the Confederate attack at the Battle of Springfield on January 7–8, 1863.

Springfield women also suffered and served during the Civil War. Mary Phelps, wife of congressman John S. Phelps, and other local women took care of the body of General Lyon until relatives could come for the body. Mrs. Phelps personally took supplies by wagon to Springfield and Greene County Union soldiers during the Battle of Pea Ridge, Arkansas on March 7–8, 1862. She later helped establish an orphanage for children of soldiers killed in the war.

The Springfield National Cemetery, which now is the resting place of men and women who have served in all wars, was originally established for the interment of soldiers killed in the Civil War.

The call to arms came again in 1898 when a company of volunteers was raised to fight after the invasion of Cuba during the Spanish-American War.

Springfieldians served their country in 1918 during World War I in Europe as part of the famed Thirty-fifth Missouri Division. That unit also contained another famous Missourian, Harry S Truman Almost twenty-six hundred from Springfield and Greene County served their country during World War I.

**Major Charles Zagonyi, commanding General Fremont's Body Guards, led the attack upon Springfield in 1861. Photograph courtesy of James Joplin.**

BRILLIANT CHARGE OF GENERAL FREMONT'S BODY-GUARD THROUGH THE TOWN OF SPRINGFIELD, MISSOURI, ON OCTOBER 26, 1861.—[SEE PAGE 722.]

**Springfield was briefly occupied by Union forces on October 25, 1861, following a skirmish west of town on Mount Vernon Road. This engagement became known as Zagonyi's Charge, named for the Hungarian commander, Union Major Charles Zagonyi.**

World War II was brought close to home not only because of the men and women who served in the armed forces from Springfield but also through daily association with the wounded soldiers who were brought to O'Reilly General Hospital for treatment and convalescence. The generous outpouring of concern by Springfieldians no doubt contributed significantly to their recovery. Springfield offered soldiers from nearby Fort Leonard Wood a place to enjoy a weekend pass thanks to the USO, War Dads, Red Cross and churches. All the while, civilians coped with shortages and rationing coupons and contributed scrap paper, metal and rags in support of the war effort.

Springfield citizens were dismayed at the 1950 outbreak of war in Korea only five years after the end of World War II. Local National Guard and Reserve units were soon called to duty. Volunteers were particularly involved in aiding the American Red Cross in stemming the blood shortage caused by the war and in reactivating the USO club to serve visiting service men and women from Fort Leonard Wood.

An uneasy peace prevailed for a brief period of time as the Cold War played itself out. Springfieldians grew accustomed to air raid drills and designated bomb shelters, with their easily recognized symbols, for use in a possible nuclear attack from the Soviet Union.

The United States' involvement in the Cold War was demonstrated by the Vietnam War and made all too real as young men and women were drafted for service. The conflict in Vietnam had another lasting effect on the community; many refugees from that country sought a new home in Springfield.

Springfield residents were called upon also to serve their country in the war in the Persian Gulf, the most recent conflict in which the U.S. was involved.

This is an early view of the Springfield National Cemetery. It was established in 1867 as the final resting place for Union soldiers killed at the Battle of Wilson's Creek and other engagements in southwest Missouri during the Civil War. The cemetery was later enlarged and incorporated the Confederate Cemetery.

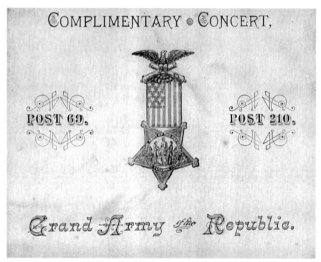

Local posts were formed for Union veterans of the Grand Army of the Republic. Veterans proudly wore the G.A.R. ribbon which is featured in this invitation.

Ben Moskowitz is representative of those from Springfield who served in World War I.

The Springfield National Cemetery today contains the remains of veterans of all wars in which the United States was involved, including one soldier from the Revolutionary War.

Closing ceremony - Booneville Ave, U.S.O. Extension Club, Springfield, Mo, Aug-11-1946

A USO Extension Club was started by African American Springfieldians during World War II to serve African American servicemen visiting the segregated city. The 1946 photograph shows the closing ceremony at the club on Boonville Avenue.

**Below:**
The War Dads operated a canteen next to the Frisco Depot where service men and women could gather while on a weekend pass in Springfield. The canteen was staffed by War Dads and Red Cross volunteers.

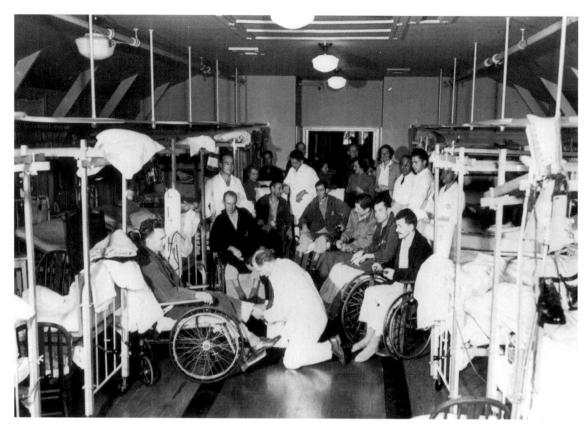

This is a view of one of the wards in O'Reilly General Hospital.

To help pass the time and to speed the recuperation of O'Reilly Hospital patients, nationally known entertainers such as the Mills Brothers visited the hospital.

**Right:**
Scrap metal was collected east of the Benton Avenue viaduct as part of the World War II war effort. The Shrine Mosque and the American Legion Hall are in the upper right corner.

Company K, composed of Springfield men, posed before beginning their 1897 practice march to Ozark, Missouri in preparation for service in the Spanish-American War.

Homes and organizations proudly and prominently displayed flags honoring service men and women during World War II. Here the *Hadassah* (meaning Sisterhood) with Rabbi Jacob display the flag from Temple Israel.

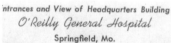

Springfield became the site of O'Reilly General Hospital, one of the ten largest army hospitals in the U.S., which treated injured service men and women during World War II. It was located on property on North Glenstone Avenue now occupied by Evangel College.

Volunteers are shown at work in city council chambers preparing to mail out ration stamps during World War II.

A group of Springfield youngsters wanted their fathers, members of a National Guard unit mobilized during the Korean War, to come home after the truce was signed.

Springfieldian Martin Fulbright (left) received the Bronze Star award in a presentation ceremony for his service in the Vietnam War.

Students in Springfield school s took part in a civil defense test in early spring. These students at Boyd School assumed the proper positions for the "duck and cover" drills which they go through regularly in addition to the regular fire drills.

Students at Boyd School took part in a civil defense test, learning to "duck and cover," during the Cold War years when a Soviet nuclear attack was feared.

A local baseball team, probably the Springfield Gas and Electric team, is pictured at White City Park in 1915. White City Park was located on Boonville Avenue where the Assemblies of God Headquarters now stands.

# 9

# An Outdoor Paradise

Drury College played the first organized football game here in 1891. In the early days of both institutions, games in football and basketball between crosstown rivals Drury and Southwest Missouri State College provided spirited contests. Both teams have claimed national basketball championships; Southwest Missouri State University won the 1952 and 1953 NAIA Championships, and Drury won the 1979 NAIA Championship.

In recent years, the SMSU Lady Bears have set attendance records at home games that exceeded seven thousand at Hammons Student Center. In 1992 the Lady Bears became the first basketball team from the state of Missouri to reach the NCAA Division I Final Four under the direction of Coach Cheryl Burnett.

Springfield was one of the first cities in the nation where softball became popular. The passion continues for softball with three hundred fifty teams now involved in softball leagues through the park program in a typical season. The National Fastpitch Softball Tournament has been held here several years, and Springfield teams have done well in the competitions.

Southwest Missouri State University's Pride Marching Band has excelled in its field. The band has been in existence for twelve years under the direction of Jerry Hoover and currently has over three hundred thirty members. They have marched in many prestigious parades throughout the country.

**Herschel Bennett of the St. Louis Browns was the first major league baseball player from Greene County. He played for minor league baseball teams in Springfield, Muskogee, and Tulsa, Oklahoma and was sold to the St. Louis Browns in 1923 for the record price of ten thousand dollars. While playing outfield for the Browns, Bennett was the fastest man on the team and held the record as a pinch hitter in the major leagues two years in a row.**

**The Springfield High School football team of 1921 posed in front of what is now known as Central High School.**

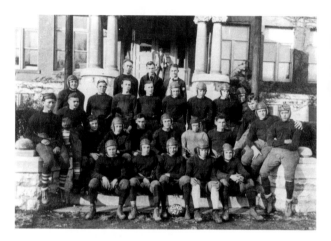

**The 1991–1992 SMSU Lady Bears went all the way to the NCAA Division I Final Four.** *Front Row (from left):* **Jim Odom, Jill Cotton, Melody Howard, Charity Shira, Amy Nelson, Tina Robbins, Secelia Winkfield, and Robin Meeks.** *Back Row:* **Head Coach Cheryl Burnett, Lynette Robinson, Angenette Sumrall, Chrissy Ediger, Heidi Muller, Karen Rapier, Tonya Baucom, Julie Howard, Jim Middelton, Marla Douglas Odom. Photograph courtesy of SMSU Photo Services**

Two members of the Hyde Park Stars baseball team are pictured with their manager circa 1950 in front of the skating rink at Silver Springs Park. They are *(left to right)*: Karl Thompson, Carl Harlow, and Robert Spencer.

Left:
Springfieldian and professional golfer Horton Smith won the first Masters Championship in 1934.

In the late 1800s Springfield joined the rest of the country in a growing love for baseball. In 1887 the Southwestern League was organized and by 1902 came to be called the Missouri Valley League. The Springfield minor league team, the Merchants, was the starting point for professional baseball in Springfield. By 1920 the team's name had been changed to the Midgets, and they were playing in the newly enlarged White City Ballpark. In 1931 the team became a Class C affiliate of the St. Louis Cardinals. The Springfield Redwings, later called the Springfield Cardinals, made their debut in April and were Western Association champions throughout the 1930s. This team produced an impressive number of fine players, including Paul Dean, Charley Breeden, Mike Ryba, Frank Howard, Mort Cooper, Walker Cooper and Stan Musial.

Stan Musial played for the Springfield Cardinals in 1941. Stan "The Man" went on to lead the St. Louis Cardinals to capture the National League Pennant, the World Series, seven MVPs and was inducted into the Hall of Fame.

Mike Ryba was one of the most talented all-around players who played for the Springfield Cardinals in the 1930s and went on to play for the St. Louis Cardinals in the famous "Gas House Gang."

In the 1920s there was also a baseball farm club of the St. Louis Browns located here, and in the 1950s a farm club of the Chicago Cubs played one season in Springfield.

Greene County had a number of outstanding African American baseball players and had a semi-pro team from 1945 to 1952, the Hyde Park Stars. They traveled throughout the area playing white teams despite threats and intimidation. These outstanding players such as Herman "Doc" Horn, Howard and Robert Duncan, the Looney brothers, Buddy Cook and Robert Spencer drew large audiences. "Doc" Horn later joined the Kansas City Monarchs, a black professional team in 1950. In seven years and several hundred games, the Hyde Park Stars lost only an estimated twenty-five contests and became a source of pride and recognition for Springfield's African American community.

The U.S. entry into World War II hit minor league baseball hard. The Springfield Cardinals did not play during the war, and the farm club was later relocated to St. Joseph, Missouri.

Springfield has also been home to several professional golfers. Horton Smith was Springfield's first professional golfer. He learned his game on the old Springfield Country Club course, located on Glenstone Avenue between Meadowmere and Portland streets. He won the inaugural Masters golf championship in 1934 and again in 1936. At the age of twenty, Smith was the youngest U.S. golfer ever named to the Ryder Cup team and played on the team seven times. During his career, Smith won thirty-three major tournament victories. He was president of the Professional Golfers' Association from 1952-1954 and was inducted into the PGA Hall of Fame in 1958. The municipal golf course located at 2409 South Scenic Avenue was named for him. Another native Springfieldian with ties to the Masters was Herman Keiser. He won the tournament in 1946, its first year of post-war play.

Payne Stewart is also one of Springfield's great golfers. Stewart won the 1991 U.S. Open, the 1989 PGA Championship, and has nine tour victories to his credit. He played on the Ryder Cup team four times and the World Cup team twice. The golf course at U.S. Interstate 44 and Glenstone Avenue was recently renamed the Bill and Payne Stewart Golf Course for him and his father, who was also an outstanding golfer.

Members of the James River Club enjoyed a July, 1915, barbecue.

Sequiota Park and fish hatchery near Galloway was a popular weekend retreat accessible by a unique Frisco electric train.

The exciting and potentially dangerous "Shoot the Chutes" ride descended into Doling Park Lake.

The *Lion in a Cage* was carved by Nathan Edward Galloway for the 1915 World's Fair in San Francisco. The life-sized African lion in a cage is carved from a single solid piece of sycamore. Originally it was displayed at Doling Park and later was moved to Dickerson Park Zoo for display, its current site. In 1992 it was refinished by zoo staff and the Springfield Wood Carvers Association. Photograph courtesy of Dickerson Park Zoo.

The dedication of the new Cooper Tennis Complex by Billie Jean King in May of 1996 brought professional tennis to Springfield. The Lasers are a franchise of World Team Tennis whose players have all won world titles. Their first season began with such stars as Martina Navratilova, Trevor "Tank" Kronemann and David McPherson. This team is the first publicly owned franchised professional sports team in Springfield.

Springfieldians have always welcomed opportunities to enjoy themselves and have found a number of ways to do it. The James River was, and still is, a popular spot for relaxing. Many have enjoyed a trip, by street car or train, to one of the private recreational areas surrounding the community. One of these was Sequiota Park southeast of town which later became a state fish hatchery and is now a public park. It was a good place to relax, and part of the fun was just getting there by the Frisco train to the Galloway station.

Doling Park opened in 1907 and offered many attractions including an exciting boat chute and later, amusement rides and a skating rink. Development of Fassnight Park came in 1925.

The first park commission was formed by the city in 1913. At that time it had only two parks to administer, Lafayette and Washington Park, both of which were part of North Springfield when the consolidation came in 1887. Both are now included on the city's historic sites register.

**Right:**
**The Ozark Greenways Rails To Trails project recently opened the Frisco Highline Trail to walkers, bikers, and horseback riders. Photograph courtesy of Ozark Greenways.**

This was a turn-of-the-century Drury Academy track team. *Left to right at top:* Charles Coon and Charles H. Wilson. *Middle:* Jim Delancy, Ted Kearney, and Will Hall. *Bottom:* Joe Edy and Charles Walker.

Springfield has had several tracks for horse racing through the years. This track, called Driving Park Place, was often used to race trotting horses. It was located on the north side of East Grand Street between Kimbrough and Kings avenues.

The next step in parks development was the purchase of Phelps Grove Park. It served as the city's zoo until 1923 when the city purchased property from the Dickerson Estate, where the animals from Phelps Grove were soon relocated. During the late 1920s and 1930s various federal programs helped build up Dickerson Park Zoo. Little was added from that time until the mid 1970s when the zoo had fallen into such disrepair that consideration was given to closing it. A revitalization effort was launched, and Dickerson Park Zoo was saved. The zoo has achieved fame for its species survival plans with notable births and scientific contributions relative to endangered species, among them Asian elephants, maned wolves and cheetahs. They have added new facilities and exhibits which have resulted in naturalistic animal attractions and increased services.

Silver Springs Park was purchased in 1938 for use by the African American community. It was equipped with a swimming pool, tennis court, ball diamond, playground equipment and a community building.

Fishing in many area lakes and streams has been a necessity of life as well as an enjoyable pastime since the earliest inhabitants came to the Ozarks.

The Victorian gazebo at Maple Park Cemetery is a beautiful reminder of Springfield's architectural past. The structure pre-dates the cemetery which opened in 1875 and was most likely built around 1870 on property owned by the Crenshaw family. The park-like area was used for picnics, band concerts, and also had a track for horse racing. The Crenshaws later donated the property for Maple Park Cemetery.

Rides at White City Park included a roller coaster and "Jack Rabbit" ride as well as a baseball field.

In the years that followed there has been much development and expansion to the city parks and recreation system. It includes fifty parks, three community centers, a day camp, sixteen softball fields, seven swimming pools and Dickerson Park Zoo.

Ozark Greenways was founded by a group of private citizens in the Springfield area who work to conserve natural resources, expand opportunities to enjoy them, and to make greenways a reality. Their first project is the South Creek/Wilson's Creek Greenway; another project, the Frisco Highline Trail, will develop a horse and bicycle trail on an abandoned rail line.

In 1912 Phelps Grove Park had this impressive entrance off South National Avenue.

The Springfield Conservation Nature Center is located in southeast Springfield and provides many educational and recreational facilities for thousands of visitors annually. Photograph courtesy of Springfield Conservation Nature Center.

The Springfield High School Orchestra with Music Supervisor R. Ritchie Robertson posed outside their school circa 1920.

# 10

# Entertaining the Ozarks

The citizens of Springfield have long shown a love of the arts and entertainment. The first vestiges of the city's culture were seen in the theaters that sprang up in the 1870s, 1880s and at the turn of the century. The first large theater was the Mansfield Opera House on South Avenue, opening in the 1870s. Famous suffragist leader Susan B. Anthony spoke there in 1875.

The Perkins Grand Opera House opened at Boonville Avenue and Central Street in 1888 and was followed by the Baldwin Theater on St. Louis Street in 1891. Also popular during this period were the Doling Park Theater which featured live vaudeville shows and the Landers Theater on Walnut Street, now the home of the Springfield Little Theater.

In the 1920s and 1930s other forms of entertainment came to the Queen City of the Ozarks. Springfieldians enjoyed popular motion pictures as well as live entertainment at the Gillioz Theater on St. Louis Street (currently being restored) and the Electric Theater on the public square. Commercial Street in north Springfield was home to the Happy Hour Theater and the long-lived Princess. Drive-in theaters, such as the Springfield Drive-In, became popular in the 1950s. By the 1980s, the trend was toward multiplex theaters.

The Shrine Mosque on the corner of St. Louis Street and Kimbrough Avenue was dedicated in 1923. At the time of its building, it claimed to have the largest auditorium west of the Mississippi River. This large auditorium provided a new location for national entertainers to perform in Springfield. The Democrats and Republicans held their state conventions in the mosque in 1924, and John Philip Sousa directed a concert there the same year. The mosque has been host to such personalities as Frank Sinatra, Glenn Miller, Elvis Presley, and political leaders such as Harry Truman, Adlai Stevenson and Richard Nixon.

The Baldwin Theater, at 318–322 St. Louis Street, opened in 1891 and burned to the ground on January 6, 1909.

The Landers Theater at 311 East Walnut Street is pictured in 1912. The brick and terra cotta theater was built in 1909 and has since been in continuous use as a venue for live drama or motion pictures. The first talking motion picture in town opened there on June 23, 1928. The Landers became the home of the Springfield Little Theater in 1970 and has undergone extensive restoration.

This is a souvenir program from the grand opening of the Baldwin Theater on December 26, 1891. The large building contained an auditorium to seat fifteen hundred, fifty-one offices, and two stores.

Other structures which have served the arts and entertainment community over the years include the 1913 Convention Center, Central High School Auditorium, Clara Thompson Hall at Drury College and McDonald Arena and Hammons Student Center on the Southwest Missouri State University campus and more recently Juanita K. Hammons Hall for the Performing Arts.

The nationwide popularity of bands and orchestras was reflected in Springfield in the 1920s and the 1930s as R. Ritchie Robertson's Boy Scout Band gained national fame as the "world's largest" Boy Scout band with over four hundred members. While Director of Music for the Springfield Public Schools, Robertson founded the Kiltie Drum Corps, said to be the country's first girls' drum corps. Robertson's son James P. Robertson, also a musician, became the first conductor of the Springfield Orchestral Society founded in 1934, today known as the Springfield Symphony.

In 1928 the Springfield Art Museum opened on the second floor of the Springfield Public Library, today's Main Library at Central Street and Jefferson Avenue. Supported largely by women of the Southwest Missouri Museum Associates, the museum grew and moved to City Hall in 1937. The Art Museum received support through a city council approved levy in 1946. With help from the community, the SMMA raised enough money to build a permanent building for the museum in Phelps Grove Park, dedicated in 1958. A new section, the Jeanette L. Musgrave Wing, was added in 1995.

**The Fellini Motor Company Show was held at the Shrine Mosque, circa 1925. The most expensive vehicle cost $695.**

**R. Ritchie Robertson was the Director of Music for the Springfield Public Schools in the 1920s and 1930s. He founded the "world's largest" Boy Scout Band and the Kiltie Drum Corps at Springfield High School.**

**Construction of the Abou Ben Adhem Shrine Mosque Auditorium at St. Louis Street and Kimbrough Avenue towered over the city in 1922.**

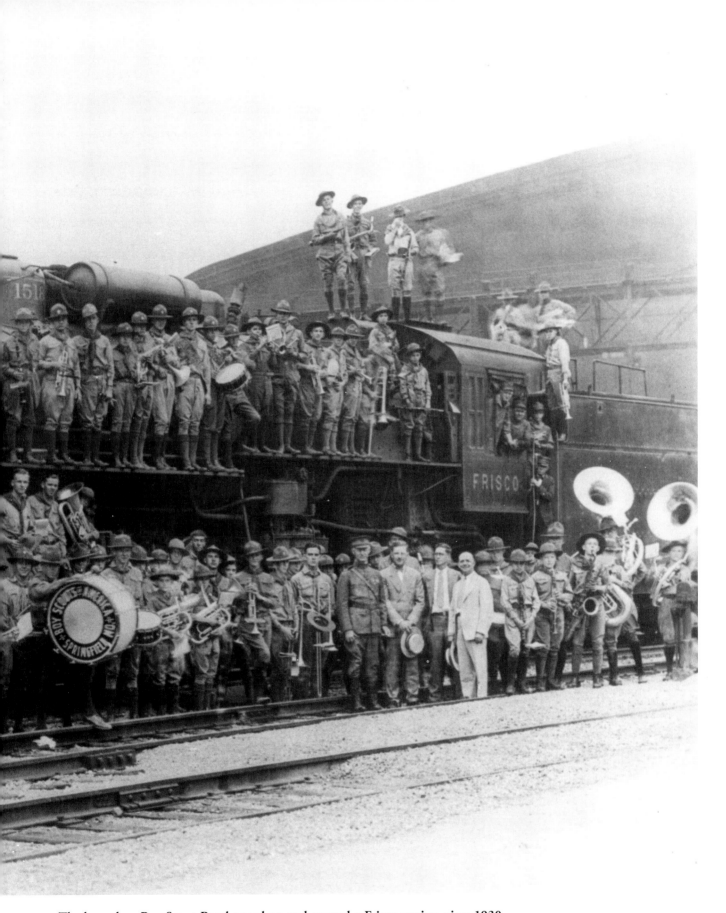

The legendary Boy Scout Band posed on and around a Frisco engine, circa 1930.

The History Museum for Springfield-Greene County began in 1975 as the Bicentennial Historical Museum. This museum was first located at 310 College Street, just west of the square, later moving into the historic Bentley House on Calhoun Street and Washington Avenue. Today the museum is located in the spacious galleries on the third floor of the historic City Hall Building.

Radio came to Springfield in the 1930s. KGBX, Springfield's first radio station, began in 1932. KWTO, founded in 1933, broadcast live performances of local and regional musicians, displaying the unique type of music that had developed in the Ozarks. Local celebrity, May Kennedy McCord, recorded and broadcast songs and folklore from the Ozarks tradition on her popular KWTO radio show, "Hillbilly Heartbeats of the Air," which debuted in 1944.

Live performances on radio led to the stage of the Shrine Mosque, with production of the show "Korn's-A-Krackin'." This early country music and humor show was succeeded by the popular "Ozark Jubilee."

**The Jeanette L. Musgrave wing is a new addition to the Springfield Art Museum at 1111 Brookside Drive. Photograph courtesy of Springfield Art Museum.**

**The Bicentennial Historical Museum in 1975 was located at 310 College Street. Today the museum is located on the third floor of the historic City Hall building.**

**Left:**
**May Kennedy McCord hosted a radio program on KWTO in the 1940s. "Hillbilly Heartbeats of the Air" highlighted traditional Ozarks music and folklore.**

The KWTO/KGBX Ozark Farm Hour Gang, circa 1940. *Standing left to right:* Mike Dosch, Charlotte Wood, Floyd "Goo-Goo" Rutledge, Bethel "Bo-Bo" Pike, Willie Wells, and Virgil Phillips. *Seated:* Hank Hutchings, Uncle Carl Haden, Bobbie Faye, Boots Faye, and Carl "Tiny" Hunt.

The Gillioz Theater on St. Louis Street opened to a packed crowd in 1926 with the film *Take It From Me*, starring Reginald Denny, a vocal group called the Swiss Songbirds, and a pair of ukelele players from a Kansas City radio station. The Historic Register theater is being restored by the Springfield Landmarks Preservation Trust.

Television soon overtook radio as America's favorite form of entertainment. Local stations KOLR and KYTV began in 1953. Seeing the popularity of traditional Ozarks music on KWTO and at the Shrine Mosque, some local entrepreneurs decided to produce a television program to showcase local talent. ABC Television in 1954 bought the program they created, "The Ozark Jubilee," and it was a regular Saturday night show for six years. The program was broadcast live from the Jewell Theater in downtown Springfield. The Jewell was the former Jefferson Theater at McDaniel Street and Jefferson Avenue. Red Foley hosted the show which featured country musicians such as Porter Wagoner, Patsy Cline, Gene Autry, Johnny Cash, Barbara Mandrell and Brenda Lee.

Springfield's rich tradition of devotion to the arts and entertainment continues today. The community now supports the Springfield Symphony, Springfield Ballet, Springfield Little Theater, Springfield Regional Opera, and many other local theaters, musical groups and art galleries. New venues have opened such as the Juanita K. Hammons Hall for the Performing Arts at Southwest Missouri State University and many multiplex movie theaters. The city is now home to five local television stations and twenty-one local radio stations, including public television station KOZK and public radio station KSMU.

The Electric Theater, circa 1935, stood on the northeast corner of the public square and was later called the Fox. It currently houses the Abundant Life Ministries.

The Springfield Drive-In Theater, circa 1952, was located northeast of the new Plaza Shopping Center near the intersection of Glenstone Avenue and Sunshine Street. Corporate Center now stands on the site of the theater.

100

The female cast of the Weaver Brothers and Elviry vaudeville act, with June "Elviry" Weaver at left, is pictured circa 1935. Many of the cast were members of the Weaver family.

Below:
Apo Hsu is the current conductor of the Springfield Symphony Orchestra. Photograph courtesy of Springfield Symphony.

The Springfield Orchestral Society, 1935, was conducted by James P. Robertson, son of R. Ritchie Robertson.

The Drury College Mandolin Club, circa 1905, is shown in front of Fairbanks Hall on the Drury College campus. *Front row, left to right:* Donald Rust, Gen Kearney, Anna Miller, Kate Holbrook, unknown, and Byron Smith. *Back row:* Charles H. Wilson, Theron Catlin Bennett, Lum Hall Frey, unknown.

A rug-hooking class met at the Ozark Arts and Crafts Center, at 839 St. Louis Street, circa 1954. Classes such as this one were popular during the push to revive regional arts and crafts in the late 1950s.

The Top Hatters Dance Club, circa 1962, gathered monthly for dinner, dancing, and fellowship.

Springfieldians enjoyed a turn-of-the-century street fair on the public square.

# 11

# Queen City Happenings

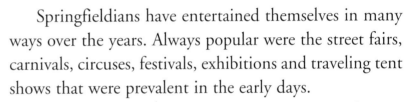

Springfieldians have entertained themselves in many ways over the years. Always popular were the street fairs, carnivals, circuses, festivals, exhibitions and traveling tent shows that were prevalent in the early days.

Some of the shows used the public square, the city lot, or other vacant areas downtown for their presentations. The circuses and fairs used fairgrounds at several locations including one near Park Avenue and Mount Vernon Street.

A Southwest district fair was established in 1856, and the fair has been a favorite entertainment for Springfieldians ever since. The Ozarks Empire Fair has been entertaining southwest Missourians since 1929 at the present fairgrounds in north Springfield, formerly a portion of the Dickerson Park property.

Springfieldians have always enjoyed parades. Some have been discontinued, but there have been parades and other forms of celebrations for Labor Day, Independence Day, Armed Forces' Day, and Veterans Day. There have been Christmas parades, homecoming parades, merchants parades, Shrine parades, circus parades and a flower parade. A parade is still held every year for St. Patrick's Day, Labor Day, Veterans Day and Christmas.

There were fall festivals, Downtown Springfield on Parade, and other significant celebrations on Commercial Street. We now have an annual Artsfest on East Walnut Street that brings thousands to the Walnut Street Historic District in May, the Firefall celebration at the Springfield-Branson Regional Airport to celebrate Independence Day and the Festival of Lights displaying millions of lights throughout Springfield for the Christmas season. To wrap up the year, many go to Park Central Square for the First Night celebration, a family event on New Year's Eve.

A number of exceptional observances are also a part of the city's history. In 1876 the national centennial was celebrated with festivities at Drury College. To celebrate Springfield's centennial a wide range of activities, including a parade and spectacular pageant, were held in 1929. In September of 1957 residents celebrated after having been chosen an All-American city by *Look* magazine. The community celebrated the country's two hundredth birthday on July 4, 1976, with special programs, activities, and a parade.

Springfield has had its share of public figures visit the city. Over the years Springfield has hosted visits from Susan B. Anthony, Elizabeth Cady Stanton, General John Pershing, Rose O'Neill (who lived near Branson), Charles Lindbergh, Henry Ford II and Laura Ingalls Wilder.

**Right:**
**Shown is the official program from the 1929 Centennial Celebration, which included an elaborate historical pageant held at the Shrine Mosque and a parade which featured the "Queen of the Ozarks," Marion Weaver Bissett and "Queen of Springfield," Mary Bryan. Both were descendants of pioneer families.**

SPRINGFIELD, MISSOURI

*Official Program*

Centennial Extravaganza

*A Pageant in Song, Story and Dance*

*Thursday, June 20th, 1929*
SHRINE MOSQUE
1829                    1929

**The annual Christmas Parade traveled down South Street, circa 1950. Pictured are Miss Merrie Christmas and her court followed by a marching band.**

**Henry Ford II visited the Ford Tractor Training Farm on the Kickapoo Prairie in the 1950s, located where Chesterfield Village stands today.**

Two Springfieldians have served as governor. John S. Phelps held the distinction of being the first four-term governor in Missouri and served in Congress for sixteen years. More recently, John Ashcroft served two terms as Missouri's fiftieth governor. He also served as state attorney general for eight years and currently serves as one of Missouri's U.S. Senators.

Located in the Republican stronghold of southwest Missouri, the city has drawn well-known politicians from both parties including many men who were presidential candidates or would later become president. The list includes such names as William Jennings Bryan, Theodore Roosevelt, Harry Truman, Thomas Dewey, John F. Kennedy, Lyndon Johnson, Hubert Humphrey, George Wallace, Richard Nixon, Harold Stassen, Barry Goldwater, Gerald Ford, Jimmy Carter, Ronald Reagan, George Bush and Bill Clinton.

Theaters have played an important role in the development of entertainment in Springfield. A number of famous performers have made an appearance in many local theaters: Fanny Brice, Lillian Russell, Mikhail Baryshnikov, George M. Cohan and Will Rogers.

Some famous performers got their start here including movie heroine Pearl White who was once a ticket seller at the Diemer Theater. The Weaver Brothers and Elviry vaudeville troupe was internationally famous. Actress Joan Crawford appeared one summer here in a stock company at the Jefferson Theater. Other natives of Springfield to make it big are Kim Crosby and Brad Pitt. In recent years, several stars of the stage and big screen have gotten their start on local campuses, including Tess Harper, Kim Crosby, Kathleen Turner and John Goodman at Southwest Missouri State University and Bob Barker at Drury College.

Throughout the history of Springfield, there have been those events that have become memorable. Many of these events are violent in nature—such events, perhaps, tend to linger longer in the memory. There have been shootouts, fires, crashes and crimes.

Laura Ingalls Wilder visited Brown Brothers' Book Store at 302 St. Louis Street in Springfield for a book signing in 1952.

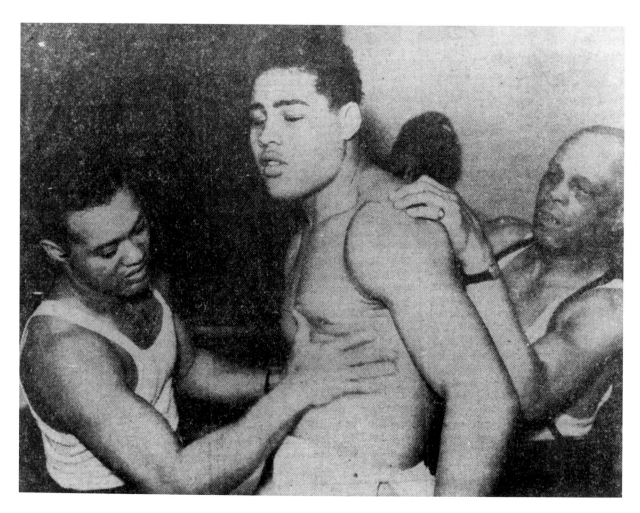

Joe Louis appeared at the Shrine Mosque for an exhibition bout with an eleven man entourage as a fund raising event for local charities in March, 1937. He is pictured here with a trainer on the left and one his managers, Jack Blackburn, on the right. The bout raised about four hundred dollars for each of its sponsors: the Child's Welfare Clinic, American Legion Auxiliary Milk Fund, the Hopewell Milk Fund, and the Negro Hospital.

In 1915 the Landers Building, now the Springfield State Office Building on the square, was inaugurated with the Human Fly climbing the ten story building. On January 2, 1932, six law enforcement officers were shot by the Young brothers, setting a record that stands today for the greatest number of police officers killed in one incident—an event now known as the "Young brothers massacre." On August 15, 1953, almost a dozen cobras escaped from a pet dealer on St. Louis Street. The city was petrified and remained indoors for two and one half months as the reptiles continued to be found throughout the community and killed. By the end of October the scare was almost over, but soon after a cobra was added to the seal of the city of Springfield to commemorate the event. In 1954 a carload of 105 millimeter shells exploded in the Frisco Railroad west yards. It resulted in a five hour bombardment of that area of town, with one person injured by shrapnel.

**Right:**
**With the SMSU Bruin Pride Band as a backdrop, President Ronald Reagan spoke to a full house at SMSU's Hammons Student Center in October, 1986. Photograph courtesy of SMSU Photo Services.**

**Former President Theodore Roosevelt campaigned in Springfield for re-election in 1912. He is shown at the Frisco Depot.**

**Right:**
**Harry S Truman appeared at the Frisco Depot during a whistle stop campaign in the late 1940s.**

The weather has always been a popular topic, and Springfield has had many remarkable weather events which are scattered throughout the city's history:

The coldest day was -29 degrees on February 12,1899.
The deepest snow was 20 inches on February 21-22, 1912.
The wettest year with 63.19 inches of precipitation was 1990.
The hottest day was 113 degrees on July 14, 1954.
The driest year with only 25.21 inches of precipitation was 1953.
The most sudden change and largest drop in temperature was 67 degrees on November 11, 1911. The high for the day was 80 degrees and fell to 13 degrees before midnight. Both the record high and the record low were set this day.

**Left:**
**Wild Bill Hickock survived an 1865 shootout with Dave Tutt on the public square in Springfield. The shootout began with an argument over a pocket watch. Tutt was killed; Hickock was tried and acquitted of manslaughter. He was killed ten years later in another shootout in South Dakota. Photograph courtesy of James Joplin.**

Springfield has been hit by several tornadoes. One of the most devastating was recorded in 1883, hitting the Grant Beach area where the woolen mill was then located and continuing east, killing seven people, injuring over thirty, and damaging at least forty structures. More recently, a tornado hit southeast Springfield in 1991, killing two people and injuring fifty-four with extensive damage.

The city has had a local weather bureau since the first official government observer came in 1887. One of the best remembered was C. C. Williford who was the weatherman from 1935 to 1956 and is credited with starting the first radio broadcasts of weather information in the country.

On Easter weekend, 1906, three young black men were taken from the county jail and dragged to the public square where they were hanged and burned beneath a replica of the Statue of Liberty. A crowd estimated at six thousand people looked on. The Missouri Militia was brought in to restore law and order. Pictured is the militia camped next to the Greene County Jail.

On June 9, 1913, the northeast corner of the public square was swept by a fire that destroyed eight buildings with an estimated loss of $800,000. The original Heer's building was destroyed and rebuilt on the northwest corner of the square on the site vacated by the Greene County Courthouse.

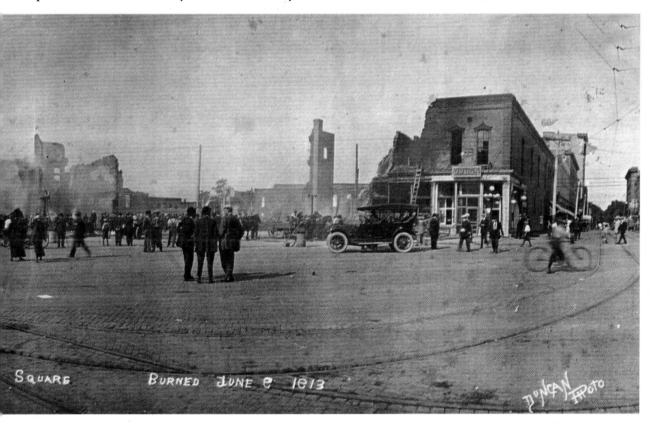

SQUARE BURNED JUNE 9 1913

DUNCAN PHOTO

On January, 27, 1933, the notorious Bonnie and Clyde made headlines by kidnapping Tom Persell, a local motorcycle policeman, when he stopped their car. He was ordered to guide them out of town and was released six hours later in Joplin, Missouri.

An American Airlines plane attempting to land at the Springfield Municipal Airport on March 20, 1955, crashed two miles from the airport. Twelve were killed instantly with twenty-three seriously injured.

112

The Jordan Creek has been flooding out businesses and residents since the first settlers built along its banks. This picture shows an area near Jefferson Avenue and Chestnut Street in July of 1909.

A thunderstorm on February 20, 1912, turned into heavy snow, dumping twenty inches on Springfield. This storm still holds the record for the most snowfall in the city's history.

Spring storms bringing tornadoes are not unusual in Springfield. In 1915 trees on the John Polk Campbell estate at Jefferson Avenue and Grand Street were devastated by a spring storm. Springfield's most recent tornado hit November 29, 1991. It caused two deaths and fifty-four injuries, destroying fifty homes in southeast Springfield. The total estimated damage was ten million dollars.

Fairbanks Hall, named for Drury College benefactor Charles Fairbanks of London in memory of his son Walter, set the scene for a student costumed celebration of the nation's centennial in 1876. The building was razed in 1978 to build the Lay Science Building.

# 12

# Preserving Our Heritage

Springfieldians have historically thought of themselves as up-to-date and in favor of progress. In our city's architecture, log homes gave way to large and stylish Victorian homes which for the most part are now only visible in photographic images. Small business buildings on the public square and surrounding blocks gradually disappeared to make room for larger, multi-story buildings, while residential areas were swallowed up by large building projects such as the Shrine Mosque and Southwest Missouri State University.

Perhaps because we have lost so much of our architectural past, there is a growing interest among Springfield's citizens in historic preservation. Efforts are being made to save and preserve buildings of historic value and local significance.

From a region of more than ten thousand sparkling springs, Springfield has developed into a community of people rich in culture and tradition. The pioneers of our community established civic, religious and educational institutions that have become rooted in the cultural fabric of the Ozarks. An atmosphere was created where Ozarks arts and culture could develop and grow. Springfield continues to evolve and meet the changing demands of today's people. As we look to the future and the decisions to be made, let us remember the traditions, hardships and accomplishments which make up our heritage and carry on the spirit of our community rich in culture and tradition.

**Germania Hall at 1144 Boonville Avenue was built in 1911 as a meeting place for *Der Deutsch-Amerikanische Bund* (German-American Alliance). The building was demolished in the 1980s to put in a parking lot. Photograph courtesy of Gary Corson.**

**Right:**
**Charles Heer constructed Springfield's largest department store at the northwest corner of the public square and College Street in 1914. The building stands on the earlier site of the Greene County Courthouse.**

After the Frisco Depot closed as a result of the end of passenger service to Springfield, area citizens began to discuss plans to preserve and use the building. However, the structure was unexpectedly demolished by the Frisco railroad in March of 1977.

The John Polk Campbell home was built in 1852, the year before his death. It stood on the Campbell farm, the site today of Jarrett Middle School at 840 South Jefferson Avenue. The Campbells raised and raced fine horses.

The John L. Holland home at 455 East Walnut Street is pictured with the owner on the front porch. The street number has been changed to 505, and the Missouri Employment Security Office stands there now.

One of the last survivors of many fine homes on St. Louis Street was built in 1902 for Mr. and Mrs. Horace B. McDaniel. This neo-Georgian style house was torn down in the mid–1960s. The site is currently a parking lot between the Hammons Tower and the Greyhound bus terminal.

# Bibliography

Barrett, Paul W. and Mary H. Barrett. *Young Brothers Massacre*. Columbia, Mo.: Univ. of Missouri Press, 1988.

Bartee, Wayne. *A History of the First Basptist Church, Springfield, Mo., 1852-1977*. Tallahassee: Rose, 1978.

Chapman, Carl H. and Eleanor F. *Indians and Archeology of Missouri*. Columbia, Mo.: Univ. of Missouri Press, 1978.

*City Directories of Springfield*. Springfield, Mo. Selected Years.

Ellis, Roy. *Shrine of the Ozarks: a History of Southwest Missouri State College, 1905-1965*. N.p., 1968.

Escott, George S., comp. *History and Directory of Springfield and North Springfield, Missouri, 1878*. Reprint. Springfield, Mo.: Ozarks Genealogical Society, 1996.

Fairbanks, Jonathan and Clyde Edwin Tuck. *Past and Present of Greene County, Missouri*. 2 vols. Indianapolis: A.W. Bowen & Company, 1915.

Grace Methodist Church. *Centennial Story, 1864–1964*. Springfield, Mo., n.d.

Grosenbaugh, Dick. *A Million Hours of Memories*. Springfield, Mo., 1979.

——. "So That All May Learn." Springfield, Mo., September, 1995.

The History Museum for Springfield-Greene County. *Crossroads At the Spring*. Text for permanent exhibit. Springfield, Mo., 1995.

Holcombe, R.I., ed. *History of Greene County, Missouri*. St. Louis: Western Historical Company, 1883.

Holland, Antonio F. and Gary R. Kremer. *Missouri's Black Heritage*. Columbia, Mo.: Univ. of Missouri Press, 1993.

Lederer, Katherine. *Many Thousand Gone: Springfield's Lost Black History*. Springfield, Mo., 1986.

Meyer, Duane G. *A Brief History of First and Calvary Presbyterian Church, Springfield, Missouri*. N.p., 1987.

——. *The History of Missouri*. St. Louis, Mo.: River City Publishers, 1982.

*One Hundred Years of Judaism in the Ozarks, 1893–1993*. Springfield, Mo., 1993.

Pearson, J. W., ed. *The History of St. Paul Methodist Episcopal Church, South 1831–1924*. Springfield, Mo., 1924.

Rafferty, Milton D. *The Ozarks Land and Life.* Norman, Ok.: Univ. of Oklahoma Press, 1980.

Schoolcraft, Henry R. *Schoolcraft in the Ozarks.* Van Buren, Ar., 1955.

Slavens, Luther J. *Biography of Rev. James Hervey Slavens, M.D. and an Autobiography.* Mary Slavens Thurston, comp. Anne and Sheldon Slater, February, 1987.

Spears-Stewart, Reta. *Remembering the Ozarks Jubilee.* Springfield, Mo.: Stewart, Dillbeck, and White Productions, 1993.

Springfield Chamber of Commerce. *The Growth of a City, Springfield.* Springfield, Mo., 1942.

*Twentieth Annual Report of the Board of Directors of the Public Schools of Springfield, Mo., with Rules and Course of Study, July 1st, 1887.* Springfield, Mo., 1887.

### Booklets

The Frisco Railroad Museum, Incorporated. "A History of the Frisco Lines, 1849–1980." Springfield, Mo., 1991.

Sheppard, Charles. "Watch Out! The Campbells Are Coming." Springfield, Mo., 1993.

U.S. Department of the Interior. *Trail of Tears National Trail Study.* 1986. Washington, D.C.: Government Printing Office.

### Articles

Gilmore, Margaret Kelso. "Family History." *The Genealogical Helper,* 1962.

Owen, Sarah Rush. "Kickapoo My Beautiful, Early Settling of Springfield." *Leader,* 3 August 1876.

### Newspapers

*Leader.* Springfield, Mo. Selected Articles.

*The News-Leader.* Springfield, Mo. Selected Articles.

*Springfield Daily News.* Springfield, Mo. Selected Articles.

*Springfield News-Leader and Press.* Springfield, Mo. Selected Articles.

# Index

cobras, 109
Cohan, George M., 107
Cold War, 77
Coleman, Arah, 70
Collegiate and Normal Institute, 48
Commercial Club, 54
Community Chest, 65
Community Hospital, 67
Company G, Third Missouri Mounted Volunteers, 13, 75
Company K, 81
Conco Companies, 33
Confederate Cemetery, 78
Congregation Share Zadek, 29
Congregational Church, 53, 58
Convention Center, 95
Convention Hall, 23
Cook, Buddy, 87
Coon, Charles, 89
Cooper Tennis Complex, 89
Cooper, Mort, 87
Cooper, Walker, 87
Cornerstone Church, 52
Corporate Center, 100
Council of Churches of the Ozarks, 60, 63
Cox South Hospital, 67
Cox, Lester E., 67, 69
Crawford, Joan, 107
Crenshaw family, 90
Crosby, Kim, 107
Crosslines, 60, 73
Cumberland Presbyterians, 57
Curtis, E. C., 70
Curtis, E. C., Mrs., 70

**D**

Dailey, Mary Bertrand, Sr., 68
Dan King's Restaurant, 27
Danforth, Mary, 12
Darton, Thomas, 70
Dayton Rubber Company, 32
Dean, Paul, 87
Delancy, Jim, 89
Delaware (Indian), 10
Delaware (tribe), 9
Denny, Reginald, 99
*Der Deutsch-Amerikanische Bund*, 28, 116
desegregation, 20
Dewey, Thomas, 107
Dickerson Estate, 90
Dickerson Park Zoo, 31, 90, 91, 105
Diemer Theater, 107
Dingledein, Sebastian, 26
Doling Park, 42, 88, 89, 93
Dosch, Mike, 99
Douglass School, 51
Downtown Airport, 20, 43, 107
Draughon Business College, 54, 55
Drive-in theaters, 94
Driving Park Place, 89
Drury Academy, 89

Drury College, 53, 58, 67, 85, 95, 102, 106, 114
Duncan, Howard, 87
Duncan, Robert, 87

**E**

Eckert, Mary, 73
Edy, Joe, 89
Electric Theater, 94, 100
Empire Bank, 32
Evangel College, 54, 62, 82
Evangelical Lutheran Trinity Church, 60

**F**

Fairbanks Hall, 102, 114
Fairbanks Spring, 57
Fairbanks, Charles, 114
Fairbanks, Jonathan, 47, 49
Fairbanks, Walter, 114
Farthing, Nancy, 73
Fassnight Park, 89
Faye, Bobbie, 99
Faye, Boots, 99
Federation of Women's Clubs, 72
Ferguson, Frances, 73
First and Calvary Presbyterian Church, 58, 66
First Baptist Church, 58, 62
First Christian Church, 48, 58
First Congregational Church, 58
First Cumberland Presbyterian Church, 58
Flynt, Larry, 67
Foley, Red, 99
Ford, Gerald, 107
Ford, Henry, II, 106, 107
Fort Leonard Wood, 77
Fort No. 4, 76
Franciscan Villa, 68
French, R. T., 32
Frey, Lum Hall, 102
Friends in Council, 72
Frisco Building, 49
Frisco Depot, 36, 64, 79, 109, 117
Frisco Railroad, 26, 29, 39, 71, 89, 97 109
Fulbright, Martin, 80
Fulbright, Ruth, 12
Fulbright, Samuel, 12
Fulbright, William, 11, 12

**G**

Galloway, Nathan Edward, 88
Gas House Gang, 87
Georgia, 13
German-American Bank, 28
Germania Hall, 28, 116
Gibson Chapel, 58
Gideon, W. G., 31
Gillioz Theater, 94, 99
Gipson, Leslie, 70
Glynn, Robert, 67
Goldwater, Barry, 107
Goodman, John, 107

# About the Editors

The History Museum for Springfield-Greene County is a not-for-profit organization, established in 1975 to collect, preserve, and exhibit the unique and rich heritage of Springfield and Greene County, Missouri. The Museum houses permanent local history exhibits and rotating exhibit galleries in Springfield's historic City Hall building. The Museum's Archives contain more than 30,000 images and documents from our community's beginnings. The Museum recently received the prestigious Award of Merit from the American Association for State and Local History.

*Photograph courtesy Barb Rogers*

Shanna Boyle, Executive Director of the History Museum, grew up in Springfield and has lived there for the last six years. She has worked for the Museum since 1992. Boyle graduated from William Jewell College with a B.A. in Psychology and an emphasis in Business. She is an active member with many local history organizations. She and her husband, Les, have two children, Shaylyn and Hayden.

Julie March, Curator of the History Museum, is a native Springfieldian and has worked for the Museum since 1982. March has B.A. and M.A. degrees in history from Southwest Missouri State University and also serves as an Adjunct Instructor of American History with the university. She is active in a number of state and regional museum organizations and chairs the Springfield-Greene County Archives Consortium. She and her husband, Curtis, have six children.

The editors gratefully acknowledge the assistance of Hayward Barnett, Patsy Corbett, Rex Edmonson, Ken Elkins, Jean Fulbright, Richard Grosenbaugh, Beth Snow and Holly Bowdidge Stone in researching and writing this book.